SILURES

RESISTANCE,
RESILIENCE,
REVIVAL

SILURES

RESISTANCE, RESILIENCE, REVIVAL

RAY HOWELL

i Jadwiga am bopeth;
David a Hannah, yn arbennig ar gyfer y lluniau;
a Maia and Hailee, a anwyd yma yn Brynheulog,
ym ngwlad y Silures.

First published 2022

The History Press
97 St George's Place, Cheltenham,
Gloucestershire, GL50 3QB
www.thehistorypress.co.uk

British Library Cataloguing in Publication Data.
A catalogue record for this book is available from the British Library.

ISBN 978 0 7509 9864 2

Typesetting and origination by The History Press
Printed and bound in Great Britain by TJ Books Limited, Padstow, Cornwall.

Trees for Life

Contents

Introduction

Just over a decade ago, I wrote a book called *Searching for the Silures: An Iron Age Tribe in South-East Wales*. It was published by Tempus in 2006 and subsequently reprinted, with minor tweaks and updates, by the History Press in 2009. Now, more than ten years later, I've decided that it's time, in light of new research and new thoughts, to revisit the investigation of the Iron Age peoples of south-east Wales.

In part, this is a response to the Covid lockdown of 2020 – but only in part. The notion of huge amounts of time generated by the lockdown has not materialised, at least not here at Brynheulog. With many board and committee meetings held by means of the once novel, now commonplace, medium of Zoom, and plenty to do in the woods and fields on the smallholding where I live, the opposite has been the case. Nevertheless, the lockdown has provided an excuse for pressing on with something that has been on my mind for some time.

This book is a departure in several respects. One is that, freed from the prescriptive restraints of things like the Research Assessment Exercise, I don't feel compelled to write formally, in the third person with copious footnotes – I'll simply report what I and others have been doing with regard to the study of the Silures and invite you to join in consideration of what new evidence and new approaches may mean. I've also decided to put notes, with bibliographical references where helpful, at the end of the book to help 'maintain the flow'.

In starting to write, I was reminded of a *Time Team* episode from not so very long ago. I'd been involved in several programmes for the Channel 4 UK series and had enjoyed doing them but I was particularly pleased when a producer rang to see if I'd come on board for a hillfort episode to be filmed near Cardiff. He said 'We'd like to have you as our Silures expert'!

I definitely liked the sound of that. I had written the first book but didn't really put myself in that category. I was flattered to think that they wanted to. Needless to say, I agreed straight away.

Filming was fun but, as usual, it was also quite hard work and the first day was a long one. I didn't live that far from the site and had decided to drive in early but spend the nights at home. That evening as I entered the village and started up the hill to Brynheulog I felt one of those 'magnetic tugs' – you may have experienced them. They draw you toward the village pub!

It was a quiet night with only a few locals in. After an exchange of pleasantries, John, who was keeping the pub at the time, announced that he had a new guest ale on, asking if I wanted to try it. My response was that I wasn't sure – what was it? It turned out to be the Celt Brewery's new offering called Silures!

I took that as fate and said yes, I'd definitely better have a pint of that. But the best was still to come. As he pulled the pint, John mused 'funny name – do you know anything about it?' Well, there's an invitation. Inevitably there followed a little chat over the bar about Silures. There is a sense in which that's exactly what I want to do in this book. Let's have a not overly academic chat – you'll have to provide your own pint.

It is important to stress that in this 'chat' we will be looking for what a range of evidence *might* mean. The Silures remain an 'open book' in many respects and, no doubt, will continue to do so. This is not a comprehensive or definitive study – it is an exploration of possibilities. The last book was 'searching for the Silures'; this one is not a volume that we can call 'Silures, found them!'

Through the years I have spent a lot of time marking Iron Age study essays by undergraduates; I often thought it would save time to have a stamp made saying 'No it doesn't'. It could have been used every time that a 'this shows that', 'this proves that', 'this makes it clear that' appeared with some explanation or another. Archaeological evidence seldom proves – it tends to indicate. We are trying to find the best explanations that we can that are consistent with the evidence presently available. That is what this volume will endeavour to do.

Before moving on, I had better note that undergraduate essays weren't always filled with attempts to leap to unwarranted conclusions. Some were incisive and interesting. Others were just interesting for different reasons. I remember fondly essays like the one that informed me that in Britain, Iron Age sites were often 'surrounded by steaks'! Sounds tasty but, while the Silures may well have managed a stake or two, I'm not convinced about that.

A final introductory note is worth stressing. In many of the chapters to come, we will be thinking about the structure of this society. That may seem ambitious – possibly overly ambitious. However, I like the idea of examining 'structures of society'. There are huge gaps in our understanding of the lives of the Silures. The limitations of our understanding of the structures of their society are even greater.

Despite what is in many instances a glaring lack of evidence, I've increasingly become convinced that trying to tease out what we can about the social structure of these people offers one of our best avenues to understanding them better.

This will be a main objective of the text that follows. I used to start Iron Age modules by telling students, 'You will find that the answer to many of your questions is we don't know. If you find that frustrating you might prefer a different module; if, like me you find it challenging and exciting, you should enjoy this one.'

There will be a similar challenge for the reader. Hopefully, you will be happy in the knowledge that we will be dealing with balance of probability in an effort to understand these people better. If you're up for that, read on.

1

Tacitus plus

The best starting point for a discussion of the Silures is the historical record. In at least one respect that doesn't take too long as our written record of the tribe, or possibly more accurately tribal confederation, consists only of the writings of the Roman historian Cornelius Tacitus and a handful of later inscriptions.

Relying on a single source is never comfortable, especially when that source seems likely to be one-sided and, to a greater or lesser extent, biased. At least Tacitus was 'in the know' – he was eventually a senator, a consul and a provincial governor. Besides, we have to turn to him because he is the only conventionally historical source available.

He was also, as far as we can tell, not only well informed but also quite balanced. After all, in a speech that he attributed to a leader named Calgacus, urging on his forces before the Battle of Mons Graupius in Scotland, he describes the Romans as 'creating a desolation and calling it peace'! What makes that description a bit surprising is that the Roman general commanding was none other than Gnaeus Julius Agricola, who happens to have been Tacitus's father-in-law.

There is another issue that will concern some historians. Tacitus refers to the Silures in three of his books. These include the *Agricola*, which describes the exploits of his father-in-law, and his two main historical works, *The Histories* and *The Annals of Imperial Rome*. It is generally thought that both the principal historical works were written between about AD 98 and AD 105, in other words up to half a century after the events described in the territory of the Silures. So, we have accounts written at some distance from the events, quite some time after they occurred, by a potentially prejudiced source. Nevertheless, Tacitus gives us a useful, and at times vibrant, account and, as you have seen, it is the only one we have – so let's run with it.

Caratacus, Caractacus, Caradog

The story of the Silures and their resistance to the advance of Rome should be put into its wider context. The initial Roman invasions of Britain, led by Julius Caesar himself, came in 55 and 54 BC. While he achieved some limited success against south-eastern tribes like the Catuvellauni, the campaigns were hardly a resounding victory and the subsequent Gaulish rising led by Vercingetorix put paid to further interventions in the short term. Arguably, Caesar's more important achievement was brought about by his campaign against, and eventual victory over, the Veneti, a powerful Breton tribe that, with a well-established maritime tradition and a fleet of ships to match, controlled much of the trade to, among other places, Britain. The destruction of the Venetic fleet forced a new trading pattern onto British Iron Age communities.

The allure of conquest in Britain, however, did not disappear. It was certainly an appealing objective in the mind of Claudius, an unlikely emperor in need of a military success. When he launched his attack across the Channel in AD 43 he left little to chance. A huge invasion force led by the general Aulus Plautius was made up of four legions including three re-assigned from the Rhine frontier. The Second Augustan, commanded by the future emperor Vespasian, would one day be permanently based in south-east Wales. These legions were supported by auxiliary forces including cavalry and specialist archers. In total, some 40,000 troops were deployed in the campaign.

Not surprisingly resistance came, in the first instance, from the Catuvellauni. They were led by two brothers, Caratacus and Togodumnus, sons of Cunobelinus, Shakespeare's Cymbeline (don't be confused by the plot of the play, which is, after all, fiction!). Preliminary skirmishing ended with a pitched battle, probably fought in the Thames Valley at a crossing point on the river Medway. Heavy losses by the Catuvellauni included Togodumnus, and with this defeat resistance in the south-east quickly collapsed. Caratacus, however, was determined to carry on fighting and withdrew toward the west with his remaining forces. He finally paused in the territory of the by now divided Dobunni, halting in an area controlled by a faction of the tribe still hostile to the Roman advance, possibly establishing himself behind earthworks on Minchinhampton Common in Gloucestershire.

This move brought him into closer proximity to the aggressively anti-Roman Silures. Not surprisingly, Caratacus and his band soon joined them and the whole focus of the Roman military advance began to shift toward south-east Wales.

From a Roman perspective, despite initial successes, Britain remained a turbulent and often hostile land. When Publius Ostorius Scapula succeeded Aulus Plautius as governor in AD 47, he found that he had to move quickly to try to stabilise Rome's 'newest province'. He rapidly dispatched troops to put down a revolt by the Iceni in East Anglia before striking into north-east Wales, attacking the Decangi or Deceangli. Tacitus suggests that the objective was simply booty, but mineral resources and a desire to drive a wedge between the more powerful Welsh tribes of the west and south and the Brigantes, who were on the verge of revolt in the north of England, may have been foremost in his thinking.

Ostorius soon had even more pressing concerns when he learned of the arrival of Caratacus amongst the Silures. He re-directed his troops and invaded the territory of a people who Tacitus tells us 'neither sternness nor leniency' discouraged from fighting. He went on to explain that 'the natural ferocity of the inhabitants was intensified by their belief in the prowess of Caratacus' who he says was at this point regarded as 'pre-eminent' among the British 'chieftains'.

Commitment of the Roman army against the Silures forced Caratacus to make a bold move. He led his followers, now no doubt bolstered by the Silures, into mid-Wales. This seems to have been an attempt to bring the Ordovices, a tribe of north Wales who shared the warlike reputation of their southern neighbours, into the conflict. The Romans could see the danger and were determined to prevent that from happening.

With the Roman army approaching him in force, Caratacus had to decide his best strategy – flee or fight. Tacitus tells us that he decided to 'stake his fate on a battle'. Caratacus was now a seasoned campaigner used to Roman tactics and he chose his ground carefully. The position is described in detail although the site of the battle is still unknown and remains a popular subject of debate. The 1851 edition of *Archaeologia Cambrensis*, for example, featured publication of a lecture given by antiquarian and barrister W. Wynne Ffoulkes in Dolgellau; he confidently asserted that the Breidden in Montgomeryshire was the place. The editor hoped that 'the controversy on this point may now be considered, if not completely settled, yet at least considerably illustrated, – as far, perhaps, as the long lapse of time will permit'. That was a forlorn hope. Regular alternative sites have appeared and re-appeared over the following 150 years!

What we do know from Tacitus is that Caratacus chose high ground with steep slopes to one side and a river, possibly the Wye, in front with no obvious crossing points available to the Romans. The position was then strengthened as the defenders erected stone ramparts where the slope was less pronounced. Having secured the position as well as possible, they then dug in and waited for the attack. Caratacus is said to have moved among them psyching them up by saying that the ensuing battle 'would either win back their freedom or enslave them forever'. Tacitus reports that 'every man swore by his tribal oath that no enemy weapons would make them yield'.

Caratacus had chosen well and initially it looked as though the defenders might achieve a remarkable victory. Even before attempting to cross the river, frightened Roman troops proved reluctant to attack such a strongly defended position 'dismaying the Roman commanders'. However, in the end discipline prevailed and, when the order to advance was given, the river crossing was made more easily than Caratacus would have hoped. The same was not true of the subsequent attack uphill. When the Romans reached the ramparts that the defenders had erected, Tacitus tells us that 'in an exchange of missiles, they came off worse', being forced to retreat back downhill having suffered heavy casualties.

In the end, however, it was the discipline and organisation of the Roman army that determined the final outcome. The Romans re-grouped and, employing their well-tested *testudo* ('tortoise') formation, advanced again. With well-drilled units creating walls and a roof of locked shields, the legionaries, now virtual human tanks, forced their way back up the slope. The close-quarter fighting that followed their breakthrough had an air of inevitability about it. The close formation of the legionary troops supported by javelin throwing auxiliaries was too much for the defenders.

In the confusion of the ensuing defeat, many captives, including the wife and daughter of Caratacus, were taken. Caratacus himself managed to escape and, still determined to resist, fled north to the Brigantes. By this time, however, the Brigantes were divided with a pro-Roman faction wanting to reach accommodation with the Romans and an anti-Roman group wishing to continue to resist. Caratacus went to the wrong faction – the pro-Roman Brigantian queen Cartimandua surrendered him to the Romans!

Caratacus and members of his family, along with other captives, were taken to Rome. There they would have had little hope – a triumphal procession through the thronged streets of the imperial capital followed by death, as had been the fate of the Gaulish leader Vercingetorix, must have seemed the inevitable outcome. It might well have proved to be the end of the story as well. Except, as Tacitus reports, Caratacus, instead of cowering and pleading for mercy, made a powerful speech in front of Claudius himself. It was a notable performance. I've quoted parts of the speech before – it's too good not to quote key sections again.

Caratacus, we are told, proclaimed to the assembled Romans, including the emperor himself, that:

> I had horses, men, arms and wealth. Are you surprised I am sorry to lose them? If you want to rule the world, does it follow that everyone else welcomes enslavement? If I had surrendered without a blow before being brought before you, neither my downfall nor your triumph would have become famous.

The speech made quite an impression. Such an impression that Claudius pardoned Caratacus and members of his family, who effectively became pensioners in Rome. There is good reason to think that he continued to impress. Another writer, the Roman historian Dio Cassius, described him later, walking the streets of Rome and marvelling at the scale of the place and its buildings, saying: 'Can you who have such possessions and so many of them still covet our poor roundhouses?'

With that searching question, Caratacus disappears from the pages of history. Importantly for this book, however, the Silures do not.

The Silurian War

The narrative of Tacitus indicates that the loss of Caratacus made little if any difference to the opposition of the Silures to Rome. Indeed, if anything they seem to have become even more hostile to the Roman advance in the aftermath.

Tacitus reported that 'in Silurian country' Roman troops under the command of a *praefactus castrorum* were directed to build forts, presumably at this early stage marching camps to facilitate an invasion. But they were surrounded and were only saved from annihilation because commanders of neighbouring fortresses, learning of the attack, 'speedily sent help'. The beleaguered force may have been saved from being massacred but their rescue came at a very heavy cost. We are told that 'casualties included the chief of staff, eight company commanders and the pick of the men'. This quote needs a bit of interpretation to understand the size of the defeat. The *praefactus*, translated here as chief of staff, was the senior centurion; the other centurions, here called company commanders, would have been at least nominally in command of eighty legionaries (army re-organisation had reduced the century from 100 men to eighty). Tacitus doesn't enlighten us as to how many soldiers were killed, but the death of the centurions that he does report suggests a military defeat on a very large scale.

For the Silures, this victory was just a start. They attacked a foraging party, and a rescue attempt made by Roman cavalry and auxiliary infantrymen failed. It was only the intervention of legionary troops that held the attackers at bay. As night fell, we are told that the Silures simply 'faded away almost undamaged'.

Hit-and-run attacks became the order of the day. Tacitus tells us that 'battle followed battle' and concluded that 'the Silures were exceptionally stubborn'. The Silures had begun a highly effective guerrilla campaign – a war that would last for a quarter of a century.

Tacitus describes what 'were mostly guerrilla fights in woods and bogs. Some were accidental – the results of chance encounters. Others were planned with calculated bravery.' He concluded that the 'the motives were hatred or plunder'. The governor Ostorius became so exasperated by the ongoing hostilities that he suggested the only solution for such a tribe was utter extermination or transplantation to Gaul. The threat of a genocidal war of extermination seems not to have cowed the Silures. Indeed, they simply intensified their opposition.

Two auxiliary units, busy plundering native land, 'fell into a trap laid by the Silures', who sent their captives as well as some of the spoils gained to their neighbours. Tacitus was no doubt correct that their motive was 'to tempt other tribes to join their rebellion'.

This war of attrition took its toll on the Romans, including their governor. With such a string of reverses, we are told that in AD 52 'exhausted by his anxious responsibilities, Ostorius died'. The Silures, Tacitus tells us, 'exulted that so great a general, if not defeated in battle, had at least been eliminated in warfare'. The authorities in Rome will obviously have seen this as a bad situation; but, from their perspective, it was about to become even worse.

The Romans named a new governor, Aulus Didius Gallus. Before he arrived to take up the post, however, Roman forces had suffered an even more memorable defeat. The senior military commander in Britain after the death of Ostorius was the general Manlius Valens. He seems to have had the sort of idea that periodically crops up among military commanders through history – he would gain the glory by defeating the enemy before the new governor arrived. Consequently, he led a legion into Silurian territory. The Silures defeated the legion! When I'm giving a lecture about the Silures, I always like to pause and repeat that for dramatic effect – *the Silures defeated the legion*. Roman forces suffered many reverses during their imperial expansion, often at the hands of alliances of resistance groups. It isn't that often that we find individual tribes defeating a legion. Tacitus makes it clear, however, that it happened in the land of the Silures.

Perhaps unsurprisingly, Tacitus provides a fairly low-key account, simply noting that 'again the damage was due to the Silures: until deterred by the arrival of Didius, they plundered far and wide'. Nor is it clear from his description that they were overly deterred when he did arrive. The new governor seems to have decided that his options were so limited that he could only act 'on the defensive'. Tacitus clearly wasn't impressed with a strategy of simply trying to defend the frontier rather than resuming the invasion.

It was only with the appointment of a new governor, Quintus Veranius, that active intervention was resumed. During his governorship in AD 57–58 he resumed hostilities, invading Silurian territory. The incursion didn't last long. Tacitus reports that 'Quintus Veranius had only conducted minor raids against the Silures when death terminated his operations'. The Silures must have been delighted that they had seen off yet another governor. They were no doubt even more pleased when the revolt of Boudica came close to forcing the Romans out of Britain altogether in AD 60/61.

The Boudican revolt is beyond our remit here except to note that it was eventually suppressed. Unfortunately, we can't say that much more about the end of the Silurian War. Tacitus was distracted by other issues and gives us only a cursory account of the end of the conflict.

What he does tell us is that in AD 73–74 Sextus Julius Frontinus became governor, replacing Quentius Petillius Cerialis. Frontinus came straight from a highly successful military command, suppressing rebellion in the Rhineland. Eventually he would gain considerable renown in Rome itself, becoming consul three times and holding the office of *curator aquarum*, with responsibility for the aqueducts that were key to the water supply of the capital. He produced a notable two-volume book, *De aquaeductu,* in which he provided a detailed description and history of the system.

With respect to his governorship in Britain, Tacitus simply informs us that Frontinus 'subdued by force of arms the strong and warlike nation of the Silures, after a hard struggle, not only against the valour of his enemy, but against the difficulty of the terrain'. Frontinus went on to commission construction of the legionary fortress of Isca, modern Caerleon, which became the military/administrative centre for the territory of the Silures. With the emergence of Isca, war gave way to occupation and our historical account largely comes to an end.

2

Inscriptions:
What's in a name?

It would have been nice to have a more detailed account of the end of the Silurian War with some explanation and elaboration of the 'hard struggle' that occurred. Nevertheless, even the brief account of the campaign of Frontinus suggests an organised and determined opposition. There is little else in the way of historical accounts. It's true that places like Caerwent, Venta Silurum (which, as we are about to see, became the Roman-era capital of the Silures), is mentioned in sources such as the *Antonine Itinerary*, which is probably best described as a sort of third-century road atlas, and the seventh-century *Cosmography of Ravenna*. However, for the Silures themselves, we must look to archaeology. Happily, one type of artefact can provide snippets of history – inscriptions. And there is an important inscription to start with.

Three, possibly four, particularly relevant inscriptions have an association with Caerwent, Venta Silurum. Indeed, two of them are, at the time of writing, prominently displayed in the porch of the church with replicas in Cardiff at the National Museum and in Newport Museum. The most prominent, the Paulinus Stone, is large, standing nearly 4ft (1.2m) tall. It is very important in helping us understand the development of Roman Britain generally and Romano-British political organisation in the territory of the Silures in particular.

The clearly cut inscription appears on a statue base (only the base, discovered in 1903, survives). It is dedicated to Tiberius Claudius Paulinus, the legate of the Second Augustan Legion, based in Caerleon. Dating from about AD 220, it tells us that the monument was commissioned *ex decreto ordinis respubl(ica) civit(atis) Silurum* (by decree of the *ordo* or tribal senate of the polity of the Silures).

This is very important for several reasons. One is that it shows that a civitas had been established in the territory of the Silures and a tribal senate was acting on behalf of the whole of the tribal lands. As we will discuss more fully later, civitas administration was a form of devolved government that the Romans used throughout the empire. Responsibility for aspects of local administration was given over to local authorities. As much of the captured territory throughout the empire was 'tribal', in practice that meant handing some powers back to tribes, no doubt with a range of strings attached.

There is also an indication implicit in the Paulinus inscription that tribal structures were sufficiently intact among the Silures to allow this measure of devolution. As far as we know, there were only two civitates established in what is today Wales: Venta Silurum, modern Caerwent, in the land of the Silures and Moridunum (Carmarthen) in the territory of the western Demetae. It seems likely that this approach was, from a Roman perspective, less a case of achieving good govern-

The Paulinus stone, pictured in the church porch at Caerwent along with the smaller Mars-Ocelus inscription to the right, provides 'text in stone' confirming the creation of the civitas and, by implication, the resilience of tribal tradition and structures. (Newport Museum)

ment and more an attempt to shift responsibility for matters like taxation onto local communities. Nevertheless, it tells us important things about the resilience of tribal structures and survival of native identity.

It tells us something else as well. In the early third century the people of the region identified themselves as Silures. When I talk to groups about the Silures, one of the most frequently asked questions is 'What did they call themselves?' It's a good question. We only have to think of descriptions like cymry/Cymru and Wales/Welsh, or other examples from farther afield like Lakota/Dakota and Sioux to realise that descriptions used by outsiders may not always be the preferred option of the people being described.

Some 'native' alternatives for Silures have been suggested. Thomas Price (Carnhuanawc, his bardic name), for example, uses Esyllwyr in his 1842 volume *Hanes Cymru* (*History of Wales*). The source of this attribution, however, is not very clear. With the Paulinus inscription, however, one thing is. The Romans called them Silures and by the early third century they were content to call themselves that as well. I've decided to do the same in this book.

Belief in relief?

There are two other important inscriptions from Caerwent, in both cases commissioned not by the tribal ordo but by Roman citizens. One, also a statue base, was set up by a man named Marcus Nennius Romanus in return for, the inscription tells us, freedom from liability for his college. Presumably this refers to an exemption from tax for a guild or some similar association.

What is most important for us is the dedication. The statue is dedicated to Mars Lenus or ('also known as' is probably the best translation) Ocelus Vellaunis. The statue itself doesn't survive apart from 'human' feet, presumably those of the god, and the feet of a bird, probably a goose, which was sometimes associated with Mars.

Mars, the Roman god of war, was also a protective deity, which could explain an association with Lenus, a native healing god known from other inscriptions in the Rhineland, particularly the Moselle region that was home to people called the Treveri (the origin of the modern town Trier). Ocelus may have been a particularly important deity in the Silurian region. The association here is with Vellaunus, a native deity also known from an inscription found in southern Gaul.

The conflation of Roman and native deities is not surprising. The Romans were generally fairly relaxed about local religions, provided they weren't perceived as overly secretive or overtly opposed to the imperial cult. Indeed, as we will discuss later, they seem to have been keen to identify and placate local gods. The best-known example of conflation in Britain is Sulis Minerva in Bath; and Caerwent seems to reflect this tendency to combine native with Roman deities very well.

This conclusion is supported by another important inscription from the civitas capital, one which now holds pride of place next to the Paulinus inscription in the Caerwent church porch. In this case, we're dealing not with a statue base but with a small (just under 2 ft 6in or 73cm tall) inscribed altar.

There are six lines to the inscription. The lower three, which today are very difficult to make out, tell us that the altar was commissioned by a soldier Aelius Augustinus, an optio or second in command of a century. He was, we are told, happy to fulfil his vow. We will probably never know what the vow was but we are left in no doubt who the altar was dedicated to. The first three lines clearly and boldly name *Deo Marti Ocelo*, the god Mars Ocelus.

Given what we have already learned about the martial prowess of the Silures, it is not surprising to find conflation of a local deity with Mars. Interestingly, as with Lenus and Vellaunus, veneration of the god was not confined to the Silurian region. A dedication has also been found at Carlisle.

Boundaries?

The fourth inscription to consider at this point is not from Caerwent itself nor is it necessarily directly associated with the Silures. It is, however, local to the study and possibly quite instructive. Found near Goldcliff on the Gwent Levels, it is an inscribed stone now on display in the Legionary Fortress Museum in Caerleon. Not surprisingly given its find spot, it is frequently referred to as the Goldcliff Stone, although the description in Roman Inscriptions in Britain (RIB 395) as 'boundary stone of Statorius Maximus' is probably more helpful.

The inscription simply tells us that the century of Statorius Maximus, of the first cohort (presumably the first cohort of the Second Augustan Legion at Caerleon), built 33 ½ paces.

It is thought that the stone was designed to be inserted in an earthwork and presumably was associated with an embankment, wall or drainage/boundary ditch. George Boon, formerly Keeper of Archaeology at the National Museum, suggested that the boundary might have been separating the *prata*, a part of the legion's *territorium* that was dedicated to grazing, from tribal lands on the Levels.

This seems a logical conclusion. Boundaries suggest separation and if land being directly exploited by the army was being defined and delineated it must have been being separated from land belonging to someone else. Given the relative proximity of the civitas capital the most likely owner was the civitas – in other words, it was tribal land.

The Goldcliff Stone: a simple statement of fact but one that may imply a great deal about relations between the civitas of the Silures and the Roman authorities. (National Museum of Wales)

Conclusions from history

At this point we really have pretty much concluded our trawl of historical sources – we have come as far as the historical record allows. That record, however, tells us quite a lot about the Silures and what is today south-east Wales in the late Iron Age. Let's summarise.

To begin with, Tacitus tells us that south-east Wales was, at the time of the Roman incursion, inhabited by a tribe called the Silures. These people were fiercely anti-Roman and were happy to welcome a Catuvellaunian prince as a war leader during the early phase of their resistance.

That resistance, however, did not require outside assistance to become increasingly hostile to invasion. It is important to stress that the Silurian resistance to Rome was organised and remarkably effective. A war lasting a quarter of a century does not suggest a disorganised or unstructured society. Some of the guerrilla fighting described might have been ad hoc and local; defeating a legion, however, was not.

A determined and structured society seems to be mirrored in post-conquest developments. Even in the aftermath of Frontinus's victory in the mid-AD 70s, a polity survived that allowed creation of civitas administration. The civitas is implicit in the inscription of the Paulinus stone, as is a surviving tribal identity.

The people of the civitas would have had to reach a measure of accommodation with Rome. One of many issues for us to consider is the extent to which that level of accommodation varied from place to place – from, for example the capital and the countryside. Retention of tribal land on the Levels, perhaps hinted at by the Goldcliff stone, may provide a starting point for consideration of that question.

Caerwent itself probably became a comparatively cosmopolitan place. Inscriptions confirm not only Roman influence but also religious beliefs and deities with parallels in other, at times continental, native traditions. Belief is often a particularly difficult area to recover from the past, particularly without written records to act as a guide. With the Silures, inscriptions at least give us a starting point.

So, to summarise what we learn from history. The Silures were a regionally powerful society that sustained a committed and surprisingly effective military opposition to Roman imperial expansion. They remained sufficiently coherent to allow the emergence of civitas administration while sustaining local systems of belief, sometimes held in common with other Iron Age communities.

All in all, the limited historical evidence available to us at the very least whets the appetite to learn more. However, having exhausted our historical sources, there is only one obvious way to do that. We must see what archaeology, the study of material culture, can tell us. It is true that archaeology and history ask and answer different questions but at the end of the day they are different questions about the same thing: how people used to live.

The archaeological picture for Iron Age Wales is limited and patchy. There are huge gaps in what has been done and consequently what we know about this period. However, it is a slowly improving picture – at least it is a bit better than it was when I first put pen to paper on the subject.

Let's have a look and see where archaeology can take us with Silures.

3

Art and artefacts:
'The study of stuff'

For several years I taught an artefact course; I branded it 'The study of stuff', which sounded a bit catchier than some of the alternatives. It was also a good way to stress that we were dealing with material culture and what it can tell us about early societies. That's what we will be trying to do with respect to the Silures in this chapter.

What we won't be doing is an in-depth, comprehensive artefact compendium. Instead, I want to look at some particular kinds of artefacts and see what sort of insights about the Silures we can infer. As always, we are dealing with balance of probabilities.

I like the idea of thinking about art and artefacts together, especially in the context of these Iron Age residents of south-east Wales. As we will see, superficially mundane, workaday objects can be artistic in their own right. There were skilful craft workers among the Silures, and this is shown by a range of objects.

Origins

Until not so very long ago a gallery at the National Museum in Cardiff was dedicated to telling the story of early Wales through objects. It was called 'Origins' and I used it regularly with students, often taking whole classes. I wish it were still there because it did an excellent job of contextualising objects, demonstrating associations and exploring ways in which early societies in Wales drew on earlier periods in a constant process of redefinition. It is a useful approach in terms of what we want to consider next.

The transition from Bronze Age to Iron Age is an interesting starting point for gaining a better understanding of the peoples of south-east Wales. Indeed, artefact variation in Bronze Age finds may even reflect differences that found expression in the regional groupings much later described as tribes by the Romans. They reported distinctive tribal groups with the Silures in the south-east, the Demetae in the south-west, the Odovices in the north and the Decangi/Deceangli in the north-east. A case can be made for arguing that differences in artefacts reflect these entities.

Certainly, there is at least one set of objects that is closely associated with what would come to be seen as the Silurian region. Here late Bronze Age assemblages, groups of associated artefacts, are frequently dominated by distinctive socketed bronze axe heads. The sockets would have facilitated 'hafting', securing to a handle, and three distinctive ridges or ribs ran along the face of the axe. A loop extended from the 'collar' along the edge of the blade, presumably also for hafting to a handle to make a functional axe.

The combination of elements is striking and quite distinctive. Arguably even more striking is the distribution of these finds. A few examples have been found in areas like the south-west of England and there is ongoing debate about where they may have been produced. There is, however, no debate about where the large majority have been found. Significant numbers of these axes have been recovered, often in hoards, i.e. deliberately buried groups of finds, throughout modern Glamorgan and Gwent. The predominance of the finds in the region has led to them being described as 'South Wales type' axes.

Such concentration of objects in an area doesn't necessarily confirm tribal affinities but it does tend to suggest aspects of cultural cohesion within that region. The age of the objects is also interesting as it points to a period of social change. There is good evidence, environmental and other, for changes in society in Britain during the late Bronze Age. Demographic change may have been stimulated by climate change, leading to at least a measure of upland deforestation. Axes would have had a role to play here. Possibly not coincidentally, during this period we also begin to see an increase in apparently defended hilltop sites. In due course, we will have to think about what we should call these sites. For now, let's stick with what they are usually called, hillforts.

These began to appear in many parts of Britain, in some cases as early as about 1000 BC. Writing a decade or so ago I noted that the scant evidence available from very limited hillfort excavation in south-east Wales might suggest a later origin in the region. The amount of excavation in the interim hasn't improved dramatically, but there are interesting exceptions that may be quite important.

One notable exception is Cardiff University's important ongoing work on the Caerau hillfort in Ely (Cardiff), an excavation that, as explained in the introduction, I had a chance to become involved with briefly while with *Time Team* filming an episode at the site. One particularly interesting discovery is that there was early, ie Neolithic, occupation. It is too early to reach conclusions but it may well be that the hillfort phenomenon in south-east Wales, as in other regions, has earlier roots than had been thought.

Deposits in water

There is also a very important group of finds from south-east Wales directly relevant to the late Bronze Age/early Iron Age transition. The assemblage was apparently deposited in a 'watery context' at about the time that bronze was first beginning to give way to iron. It's little wonder that the artefacts were once central to the 'Origins' exhibition in Cardiff.

Llyn Fawr is near Rhigos, Rhondda Cynon Taf. When the lake was being developed as a reservoir in the early twentieth century, two riveted sheet-bronze cauldrons were found with a number of associated objects. These included bronze socketed axes, two socketed bronze sickles, bronze harness fittings and a razor. The recovery of the material over a hundred years ago was less than professional by modern standards but it seems reasonable to assume that it was deposited with, and quite likely in, the cauldrons.

The Llyn Fawr cauldron is one of our earliest Iron Age artefacts. The associated material, probably originally deposited in the cauldron, tells us a great deal about a society in transition. (National Museum of Wales)

What is especially important is that also found were a wrought iron sickle, a wrought iron socketed spear head and a fragmentary Hallstatt sword. The assemblage is thought to date from between 700 and 600 BC, a time frame right for the emergence of iron.

It is also worth noting that the iron sickle is an apparent copy of the bronze sickles found. The design is one that works well in bronze; it is not a particularly good design in iron. We seem to be presented with a snapshot of people used to bronze, coming to grips with a new material and new production techniques.

This emergence of iron use is clearly important. It isn't called the Iron Age for nothing! The apparent ritual deposition of the material in water is also instructive. Llyn Fawr is one of two well-known Welsh sites where an impressive range of objects was deposited in water. The other is a north Wales location, Llyn Cerrig Bach on Anglesey. Other similar Welsh ritual sites have been suggested, fitting well with a much wider Iron Age tradition of 'watery deposition'. Similar sorts of deposits are known from locations in Britain like Bath and in the Thames and there are parallels from the continent with, for example, deposits in the Seine.

Continental comparisons bring us nicely to the Hallstatt sword. Hallstatt is a 'type site' in Austria that has given its name to a distinctive range of iron objects that were produced in the late Bronze Age and early Iron Age. This 'Hallstatt tradition' with its distinctive style is often used to define the early European Iron Age. Its use is not dissimilar to that of the description La Tène, another type site, located on Lake Neuchatel in Switzerland, which has given its name to a decorative style widely associated with the later Iron Age in Europe.

The fact that a Hallstatt sword was found at Llyn Fawr was one of several factors that provided a stimulus for the once fashionable idea that the British Iron Age was a result of widespread migration with first Hallstatt and subsequently La Tène waves of settlement. That view is not so popular now and it is worth reminding ourselves that styles and new materials can and do move among cultures through various exchange mechanisms – you don't have to have waves of immigrant settlers to bring the changes with them.

That is probably a good point at which to pause and take stock. The evidence we have looked at so far might be encouraging you to think about it in one of two ways. On the one hand, there seems to be a large degree of cultural continuity within the Silurian region. On the other, there are also similarities in techniques, materials and ritual practice to those of Iron Age communities in other parts of Britain and beyond. What do you fancy? Immigrants bringing new ideas and techniques or a stable population borrowing ideas gained from trade and other exchanges? Perhaps, a bit of both?

The best strategy at this point is to keep an open mind. I strongly suspect that, in the main, the forebearers of the Silures of Iron Age south-east Wales were the inhabitants of Bronze Age south-east Wales. However, we need more evidence to be sure.

Everyday things?

Most archaeologists like pots – you frequently find ceramic material in excavations as well as chance finds sometimes just lying around. It may sound odd to anyone used to playful young children or who is slightly clumsy when washing up to suggest that fired ceramics are durable. By and large, however, they are. Yes, they break and often break again until you are left with small sherds, fragments – but these tend not to break and they lie around waiting to be found. What's even better is that they are frequently fairly easy to date and, if you are lucky, can tell you roughly where they were made.

As a consequence, artefact reviews often begin with the ceramic assemblages. That's sometimes not as easy as it sounds with respect to the Welsh Iron Age. For a long time, there didn't seem to be much, if indeed in some regions any at all. I have books on the shelf from the 1970s confidently describing an aceramic Iron Age Wales.

Part of the problem was probably that we simply hadn't been looking properly; at least we hadn't been digging in the right places. The picture is better now, although it does seem that there was variation in ceramic use in different parts of what is today Wales. Indeed, there may have been a fair bit of variation within the Silurian region itself.

A site where pottery was found relatively early on in excavations is Llanmelin, an interesting hillfort about a mile north of Caerwent with, among other features, a distinctive annex and a small associated outpost. It was one of two Iron Age sites investigated by Victor Nash-Williams in the 1930s. Relative proximity to the civitas capital was no doubt a factor in making both Llanmelin and nearby Sudbrook attractive as targets for research.

One type of ceramic found at Llanmelin, also found at Lydney, featured a distinctive decorative pattern with chevron and zig-zag design described as 'eyebrow decoration'. Not only was it used at the site, it has been suggested that this 'Llanmelin-Lydney ware' could have been made somewhere in the region. It was also found in the excavation of the Twyn y Gaer hillfort not too far from Abergavenny. Llanmelin-Lydney ware seems to have given way, at least in part, to a style described as South-Western Decorated Ware, which was produced in the Mendips.

There are interesting points of comparison with finds from our excavation of Lodge Hill, the hillfort that looms over Caerleon. Colleagues from the university and I were able to partially excavate the site with students in the year 2000. It was a great team with experience and expertise provided by Josh Pollard, Mike Hamilton, Adrian Chadwick, Anne Leaver, Rick Peterson and others. The pottery that we found was important, if slightly surprising.

Dominating the assemblage were ceramics from the Malvern region, including vessels usually described as 'slack-shouldered' jars with beaded decoration on the

rims. Similar finds were made at Twyn y Gaer. Other ceramic finds included jars
with flat, expanded rims that have parallels across the Bristol Channel.

Arguably the most important ceramic finds from Lodge Hill were sherds of briquetage. These indicators of trade are sufficiently significant to consider in some
detail, and we will do so in the next chapter. However, the ceramic material we
have already discussed gives us plenty of food for thought at the moment.

One thing to think about is how and for what purpose these ceramics were
being obtained and used. Sooting on some of the Lodge Hill examples suggests
that at least some of them were being used on site as cooking pots. Some were
probably produced locally. Material from the Mendips or Malverns, however, is
reminding us of something else.

As a number of the ceramic vessels on these excavations came from other areas,
the assemblages clearly indicate trade. It's never easy, or at times possible, to say
what was being traded – was it the pots themselves or whatever was contained in
the pots? Whichever, we are presented with good evidence of some sort of trade.
The Silurian region had contact with its neighbours, interacting with other areas.

The level of this interaction may have been variable within the territory of the
Silures. For whatever reason, as far as we have seen to date, ceramics seem to have
been more common in the east than in the west of Siluria. Close proximity to
large navigable rivers, notably the Usk and Wye, as well as to the coast may have
been a reason for this.

There is another important point to note. A lack of ceramics doesn't mean a lack
of sophistication or complexity in a society. There are all sorts of ways to transport,
store and utilise goods, many not always obvious in the archaeological record. No
doubt you could produce an excellent cawl in a cauldron. You can also easily store
and transport things in containers made of materials like wood and leather, which
tend not to survive. Today, for example, there has been a push to exchange plastic
bags for environmentally friendly, sometimes paper, 'bags for life'. Whether bio-
degradable or not, we are still carrying stuff around in bags! It's a safe bet that the
people in all parts of Siluria were moving, storing and utilising resources whether
we can find direct evidence of it or not.

Masters in metal

Apparent variation in the distribution, and presumably as a consequence, use of
pottery is interesting. Equally if not more interesting is an apparently much more
'universal' style within a widespread regional distribution of metalwork, one of the
most important elements in the artefact assemblages of Iron Age south-east Wales.
It is one of those elements where art and functionality combine – a resounding
confirmation of skilled artisans.

An aspect of metalwork where you would expect a large measure of artistic expression is items of personal adornment. There is quite a range from the study area, including an assortment of La Tène brooches.

As we have already discussed, La Tène style is often seen as an expression of the widespread and fairly ubiquitous culture of late Iron Age Europe. It features an array of abstract patterns often derived from plant and animal designs. A well-known example is the trisgell (triskele) design with its whirling, triple-armed imagery. In the main, such imagery is found on high-status objects, often metalwork, and there are a number of good examples from the lands of the Silures.

This La Tène style emerged in the late fifth to early fourth century BC and was rapidly adopted by Iron Age elites across Europe. The Silures seem to have embraced the style as some fifty brooches have been found on Iron Age sites throughout the region, with over twenty more coming from Romano-British contexts in the area. Other types of decorative personal objects have also been found, like penannular brooches and what are described as 'swan's neck' pins.

Many of these items were made of bronze, although iron objects have also been found. For example, we had a very nice La Tène I-type iron brooch with a mock spring mechanism on Lodge Hill. The apparent rarity of iron brooches compared with those made of bronze is probably deceptive. Bronze often survives better, particularly in the difficult soils often found on sites in south-east Wales.

Among the examples of well-crafted metalwork objects there have been other items found, although in some cases these have subsequently been 'unfound', i.e. lost! Annoyingly, examples include a bronze sword hilt cast on an iron blade that is reported to have been held in the museum of the Monmouthshire and Caerleon Antiquarian Association at some point in the nineteenth century but today we know no more about it than that.

Arguably even more annoyingly, bronze helmets, two or perhaps four, were reportedly discovered with burials at Merthyr Mawr in 1818. They were said to have been dispatched for display at the Society of Antiquaries in London only to disappear in transit. At least drawings, which are the only record to survive, may help to interpret what might have been a helmet crest knob found in the Seven Sisters hoard.

Happily, especially given the warlike description of Silures by the Romans, there is a sword recovered by excavation; a short sword with a bone pommel, a sword hilt guard and an iron spearhead were found on Twyn y Gaer. Things have improved since the nineteenth century – we still have these!

We have other things as well. I'm quite attracted by the five tankard handles, four adorned in La Tène style, from the Seven Sisters hoard. Tankard handles have also been found in Caerleon. I can't help thinking that these are giving us useful insight into the lifestyle of the Silures.

Items from the Seven Sisters hoard give us many clues about the lifestyle of the Silures. Particularly noteworthy are the items of horse trappings including terrets. Don't forget the tankard handles, which are probably telling us something else. (National Museum of Wales)

Something else that is of interest is the presence of torcs. These were neck rings thought to have been status symbols, badges of rank, in the Iron Age. They have been found in many parts of Britain and beyond. In the Silurian region, bronze fragments thought to have been parts of torcs have been found near Caerwent, Cowbridge and Sully. Another fragment from a torc or a bracelet was found at Merthyr Mawr; there may have been similarities with a similar find from Llantwit Major. It was found in 1861 and, once again, is now lost.

Torcs and brooches give a picture of personal items that fits well with the prevailing general image of 'display' in Iron Age Britain. There have also been a number of shale armlets or bracelets with examples from Caldicot, Caerleon, Caerwent, Cowbridge, Dinas Powys, Llanmaes and Loughor. Some of these may have been Romano-British objects but others seem to be from Iron Age contexts. In the main, these objects were made from Dorset shale and consequently represent another indicator of trade.

There is a point to be made in passing: shale objects are black. A number of the metal objects were enamelled and a lot of it is red. There may be a theme here. Marlies Hoerchel has argued convincingly in her doctoral thesis that these blood red colours may have had a particular appeal to a people among whom martial display was particularly important. In a moment, we will consider one of the region's most iconic Iron Age objects, the Lesser Garth terret. The red La Tène enamelled design on black may have had a particular resonance.

I hesitate to mention an interview I had with the *Western Mail* shortly after my first book on the Silures was published. I only hesitate briefly! A Wales–Italy rugby international was looming and they wanted to talk about this idea in the context of Wales/Italy, Celts/Romans, and red jerseys. I tried not to say anything that would sound too unprofessional; clearly you can't, with hand on heart, make that connection. However, it was fun to discuss the idea. It was also good that the article didn't make any outlandish claims when it was published. Besides, when I had a chat with a bookshop owner in Llanelli a week or so later, I was told that sales had increased as a consequence.

Equestrian elites?

I've mentioned the Lesser Garth terret. It is a key object in bringing us to what I think is one of the most telling metalwork assemblages from the region. To make a start, it is useful to look again at the Seven Sisters hoard.

We've already noted the distinctive tankard handles in the hoard. There is also a great deal of material relating to horses. Examples include metalwork from bridles with strap-unions, a strap-slide and bridle rings. These add to an impressive array of equestrian equipment from across south-east Wales.

A distinctive example is an enamelled bronze harness fitting from Chepstow that is decorated with an 'S-scroll'-shaped design. The S-scroll motif appears again on an example of harness trapping from Ystradowen as well as items from the Seven Sisters hoard. The similar elements in the design have led to the suggestion by Adam Gwilt, who has done much good work on the finds from the area, that this may represent a unique regional tradition, possibly made as well as used, in south-east Wales.

A key theme is emerging here. Horses, it seems, had an important role in the region associated with the Silures. This increasingly safe assumption is supported by the extent of equestrian material found right across the area usually seen as Siluria. It is particularly interesting to note the similarities in design between examples from east and west. Where variation may typify ceramics in the region, a degree of uniformity seems to have prevailed in the metalwork. And if more evidence is needed, we have the horses themselves – or, at least, representations of them in metal.

There is a nice bronze representation of a horse found near Abercarn. It is similar to another bronze figurine from Clydach. The now badly out-of-date texts from the 1970s, which I mentioned before, include an argument that the Abercarn figure couldn't really be an Iron Age object because the region was 'artefactually impoverished' in the Iron Age. Happily, we now know better.

Let's summarise: metalwork of the highest quality confirms, among other things, that horses were important in Iron Age south-east Wales. That once surprised people, perhaps in part because Tacitus didn't mention it. But there are many things he didn't mention; his was never meant to be an ethnographic study.

Moreover, there is a particularly important aspect to this equestrian tradition. To begin to understand it, we need once again to look more closely at the Seven Sisters hoard. We have seen a range of horse trappings in the assemblage. There is an important related element to add to the equation. Also present in the hoard were terrets. These were distinctive metal rings, often decorated, in some cases with striking La Tène designs. They have become increasingly prevalent in the growing assemblages from south-east Wales, with several coming into the public domain through the Portable Antiquities Scheme.

Good examples include one found in cobbling associated with the gate at the Castle Ditches hillfort near Llancarfan, another from Penllyn and an example from Black Pill in Swansea Bay. A distinctive terret found in the Roman fortress at Usk is an Iron Age design, as is a copper alloy example from near Caerleon.

All these good examples, however, seem more than a little understated when compared to the impressive terret from Lesser Garth. As we have already seen, it was intricately decorated with red enamelling on the black ring. One of my memorable moments came when *Time Team* took a group of pupils from Ely to the National Museum in Cardiff where Adam Gwilt had some suitable artefacts to be discussed during filming with the children. Suitable indeed! I found myself holding the Lesser Garth terret.

It's a big terret. It's roughly 5.5 x 4in (14 x 10cm). It's heavy and I rate it as one of the most impressive objects in the museum's large array of objects. It, along with the other terrets that have been found, probably tell us a lot about the Silures – and they certainly tell us one thing.

Terrets had, and indeed still have, one function. They are for guiding reins through. The inescapable conclusion is that these people were using horses to pull wheeled vehicles. This conclusion is confirmed by other objects from these assemblages – find sites including Penllyn, Pentyrch, St Arvans and Wern y Cwrt in Gwent have produced linchpins, sometimes accompanied by axle caps. These items secured an axle to a wheel.

The picture presented by this growing body of horse-related equipment, including wheeled vehicles, is increasingly unequivocal. Any lingering doubt has, I think, been blown away by the discovery, early in 2018, of a chariot burial in Pembrokeshire. Initially a metal detector find, subsequent excavation has recovered a terret, bridle bits, a strap union and other harness fittings, some decorated in late La Tène style, as well as the iron tyre rims that would have

The Lesser Garth terret: one of our most iconic Iron Age artefacts. The size, quality and artistry suggest 'equestrian elite' to me. Holding the terret for a *Time Team* shoot is a vivid personal memory. (National Museum of Wales)

been fitted to the wooden wheels, and an iron sword, presumably placed with the deceased.

These remarkable finds are a game-changer in terms of our understanding of the Iron Age peoples of Wales. Not so very long ago, chariot burials were thought to be a regional rite confined to Yorkshire. More recently, however, other examples have been found, including an impressive burial from Newbridge near Edinburgh. The Pembrokeshire discovery places Wales within this tradition.

Perhaps, given the range of finds from south-east Wales and further confirmatory evidence such as the iron tyre rims from Llyn Cerrig Bach in north Wales, we shouldn't be surprised. Nevertheless, it is exciting to see such impressive confirmation in the form of a chariot burial in Wales.

Of course, Pembrokeshire isn't in the territory where the Romans tell us we would have found the Silures. Nevertheless, the artefact assemblages show that, however they were interring their dead, the Silures were making good use of wheeled vehicles.

It seemed to me, given this body of evidence, perfectly reasonable to think in terms of reconstructions and I was very happy to act as a consultant for a chariot reconstruction project recently organised by Yr Hyddgen, an education group based in Cwmbrân. They were fortunate enough to be able to commission wheelwright Bob Hurford, who has built chariots, based on examples from different periods and different parts of the world, for agencies including the BBC.

I could be a little biased, but I think that what he produced, now in Torfaen Museum in Pontypool, is excellent. There were, of course, issues. At the outset, he confided to me that he was concerned that what Yr Hyddgen wanted was specifically a replica Silurian chariot. My advice was that since all that we had to go on in that respect was the metalwork, if we got that right it was the best that could be achieved. Not surprisingly, reproductions of items like the Lesser Garth terret loom large.

Now is probably a good time to consider what we should be calling these wheeled vehicles. Some modern archaeologists have been very exercised by the desire to avoid ascribing military connotations to Iron Age and other prehistoric objects. We will see this tendency when we consider hillforts. They prefer descriptions like 'cart' and 'cart burial' or 'wagon'. I've never been overly keen on this nomenclature.

When it comes to describing Iron Age vehicles, I've always been more comfortable with the Welsh *cerbyd*. After all, a perfectly good translation of *cerbydau* is 'vehicles'. When I look at an object like the Lesser Garth terret, I don't think I'm examining the trappings of a farm cart! Moreover, the discovery in Pembrokeshire makes even *cerbyd* seem a bit too tame. The artefact assemblages combined with the descriptions of Tacitus paint a picture of warrior communities. An equestrian elite seems to fit this picture very well. I think we would do well to describe at least some of these *cerbydau* as what they clearly were, so the most appropriate description is chariot.

4

Trade and commerce: Wheels and keels

One of the things that encouraged me to write this updated account is our improving body of evidence from the Silurian region. New discoveries, along with the passage of time, encourage new ways of thinking about things. The Pembrokeshire chariot represents a big addition to the body of evidence. In at least one respect, however, old assumptions still seem sound, even in retrospect. The use of wheeled vehicles, *cerbydau* including chariots, seems to me to point to a related assumption. To make wheeled vehicles work, there is something that you need: roads.

That may seem like an overstatement but I don't think that it is. Yes, I know off-roading is quite possible in the landscape of south Wales. I remember driving the Land Rover to a site by the only practical route available, i.e., with the farmer's permission, through a recently ploughed field. While I know it can be done, I don't recommend it!

I've also shown that you can try to take a cup of coffee with you on a *Time Team* Land Rover hurrying to film at a castle site located up a steep, earthen track. You can even manage to drink a little of it before showering in the rest; I don't recommend this either. There have been treks with students and equipment by quad bike – something that would have given our health and safety officer sleepless nights had he seen it.

On balance, however, none of these adventures have been efficient ways to travel. You need roads. When I suggest this, I'm sometimes challenged with – OK, where are they? It's just an idea, but I'll bet you that at least some of them are under the Roman roads that, at least in some cases, we already know about. The Romans weren't daft and they often wanted to go where Iron Age communities had already been going for quite some time.

In order to see if this is right, we're going to need to do a bit of digging. I've had a few chances to do this like the opportunity to excavate what was widely

The chariot reconstruction made by Bob Hurford. Notice fixings like the reconstructed Lesser Garth terret prominently (and usefully) deployed on what has proved to be an efficiently functional chariot. The reconstruction is currently housed in Pontypool Museum. (Rhisiart Morgan, yr Hyddgen)

The Park Farm road surface revealed and ready for full excavation. We were lucky, after a fashion, that this prime candidate for a Roman, and perhaps earlier, road produced nice datable material. Bit of a shame it was all medieval! (Ray Howell)

described as a Roman road near Caerleon, on the approaches to Lodge Hill. It looked the part but I warned the students before we started that it would be hit or miss in terms of finding dating evidence. In the event, we were lucky (sort of). There was nicely datable ceramic material sealed under the lower of two road surfaces – it was medieval! Never mind, I'm still betting on there being relevant examples just waiting for us to find them.

Below the salt?

As important as some form of roads must have been, I think we need to look at something else to explain another important bit of evidence. If we look back at ceramics, you will probably remember that some of the types found in southeast Wales were produced in other regions, including examples from south of the Bristol Channel and from the Malverns. When we discussed the Lodge Hill excavation earlier, I mentioned briquetage and promised to come back to it. Now is the time because this is a particularly important find from our excavation that relates directly to this distribution pattern.

Briquetage is a ceramic form that elicits interest not because of its beauty (it really doesn't have any) but because of its known uses. It is so crudely made that for many years it was identified in archaeological reports simply as VCP – very coarse pottery! It is, however, critical in understanding the salt trade because these crude briquetage vessels were used exclusively in the production and distribution of salt.

The two fabric forms found on Lodge Hill can both be traced to the area around the Droitwich brine springs in what is now Worcestershire. Salt production began here as early as the sixth century BC and continued until the arrival of the Romans; the Lodge Hill material spans much of this long time period, indicating a lengthy involvement in the salt trade. This is important not least because the hillfort is outside the previously known distribution range for this material.

Perhaps not surprisingly, given the assemblage we had at Lodge Hill, the southern range of this material is frequently associated with Iron Age Malvernian pottery. Interestingly, examples of Droitwich briquetage have also been found on Twyn y Gaer hillfort and at the promontory fort at Sudbrook.

Once again, this is a convenient point at which to pause and take stock. Southeast Wales, the territory of the Silures, was clearly a part of exchange mechanisms that facilitated contact and exchange with other Iron Age communities. We have just given some thought to vehicles and roads – roads may well have been a factor in helping trade to develop. However, once again we need to think about this carefully.

We know that pots and salt were arriving from what is today Worcestershire and parts of Herefordshire. We should remind ourselves that pots, even crudely made ones, are relatively heavy. When they have something in them, they are even heavier. It's worth noting that Droitwich is nearly 80 miles from Caerleon and that's as the crow flies. People might have been moving goods by road over that sort of distance – but I doubt it.

When you read accounts of pre-turnpike British roads even in the Early Modern period, you quickly begin to see why people preferred not to use them. If you wanted to move a load of trade goods including pots to south Wales from somewhere near Worcester in the Iron Age, I think your best bet would have been to put them on a boat – in this case, a boat on the Severn.

We can be really speculative and picture goods moving not just down the Severn, but also into the Bristol Channel and on to coastal centres like Sudbrook. It's also easy enough to think of transhipping goods up major rivers like the Wye and the Usk. It probably isn't coincidental that Lodge Hill is in a dominant position above the Usk. Twyn y Gaer is not that far from Abergavenny and the upper Usk.

What the presently available evidence seems to me to be suggesting is at least a measure of coastal and/or riverine trade. To make the case, of course, it would be nice to have a boat or two in the archaeological record. Unfortunately, at the moment we don't – at least not from the Iron Age. However, we do have examples that bracket it. Let's have a look at those.

Boat builders

Wooden boats tend not to survive in most archaeological conditions. One in which they can is waterlogged deposits – and we are, after all, thinking about boats. In the event, we have a few examples from the British Bronze and Iron Ages in just such conditions.

A well-known example of the former is the Dover boat, while Iron Age log boats have been recovered from sites like Fiskerton in Lincolnshire. In south-east Wales we have, so far at least, had to content ourselves with what were probably reused fragments of boats.

Planks have been found on the Gwent Levels at Caldicot and Goldcliff. In both examples, these were once sewn planks from the hull of boats. Boats with sewn plank hulls have been found at a number of European later prehistoric sites and these Gwentian examples sit comfortably within this tradition. It's a tradition that has persisted. There are still sewn vessels plying their trade in places like the Indian Ocean today – it's a construction technique that works.

Fragments of Bronze Age boats in Wales shouldn't come as a surprise. One of the best-known Welsh prehistoric objects is the Caergwrle bowl from north-east Wales, thought to date from about 1200 BC. It is a representation of a boat: the shale bowl/boat is decorated with applied gold leaf representing waves, oars, and possibly shields along the gunnels. There is a suggestion of eyes at both ends of the boat, a decorative tradition with many parallels from around the world.

There is another particularly important find from the Levels that presents us not with fragments but with an actual boat. The comparatively complete Barland's Farm boat survived to a length of nearly 32ft (9.7m) and was once almost 37ft (11.4m) long and over 9.5ft (3m) wide.

This Barland's Farm vessel, which dates from about AD 300, is a good example of what is widely referred to as the 'Romano-Celtic' boat-building tradition. The point is that the builders employed techniques that in several respects were more in keeping with indigenous northern European designs than with Roman approaches to ship building. It was a sophisticated vessel in its way; the preserved mast step shows that its crew could hoist sail when desired. As Barry Cunliffe, who has done much to clarify prehistoric Atlantic trade patterns, points out, it is one of three examples of recovered Romano-Celtic boats that could be regarded as a sea-going vessel.

The boat was excavated next to a possible jetty on the bank of a tidal creek. These 'creek ports' could have been particularly important on the Levels. The Magor Pill boat, thought to have been built in the thirteenth century, shows that the pills, the creeks, were still in use in the medieval period.

Celebrations of trade

As I cautioned when we began looking at boats, we still don't actually have an Iron Age example. But as you have just seen, we have interesting boat examples that are older and a bit later, which bracket the period nicely. We also have evidence of trading networks along the foreshore of south-east Wales. An interesting case in point is Llanmaes, where recent excavations have been undertaken by the National Museum of Wales.

Here a roundhouse with associated pits and a large midden deposit have produced a range of objects including more horse-related harness equipment, spindle whorls, fragments of bowls and of cauldrons. There are also Amorican (think Brittany) bronze axes. The material suggests active occupation of the site in the early Iron Age, from about 800 to 500 BC.

One of the most striking discoveries is the very large quantity of bone recovered. Not only was there a great deal of animal bone (some 70,000 fragments), but the nature of that bone is surprising – it was overwhelmingly from pigs. And not only that, but a disproportionate amount of the pig bone was from the right front quarter of the pig.

The unusual quantity and nature of the bone assemblage suggests quite strongly that this was a site of ritual feasting. Meat from pigs was widely regarded as being a high-status food appropriate for celebratory communal meals and it seems that at Llanmaes a particular type of joint, whether as a matter of taste or possibly as a render due, was preferred. One good reason for such feasting over such a long period could have been to mark trade. What better way to celebrate the successful conclusion of a trade mission than to have a party?

Here's a thought in passing. Feasting on the scale implied here must, you would think, mark important commercial exchanges. If some of the trade objects involved originated in places like Brittany, as the axes seem to imply, that could begin to explain the scale of celebrations. I'll leave you to decide for yourself what the shark tooth carefully placed in one of the post holes of the roundhouse might imply. Your guess will be as good as that of anyone else, I expect.

Keeping the idea of 'creek ports' in mind, there are a number of sites near the coast of south-east Wales that might fit the bill, proving to be locations not dissimilar to Llanmaes. With evidence of Iron Age metalwork and items like the La Tène brooch noted previously, the area around Merthyr Mawr Warren could be a candidate. Having been involved in programmes with *Time Team* and *Olion* on S4C in the area, I'm in no doubt about how difficult the dunes can be. Sand is not the easiest material to dig! However, finds over the years have been impressive and proximity to Traeth yr afon (beach of the river) fits the creek port theme pretty well.

In the early Iron Age, there may have been a number of trade terminals near the coast. In the early Iron Age, there doesn't seem to have been, at least on the basis of what we've seen to date, a trade terminus on anything like the scale of Hengistbury Head on the Dorset coast, which emerged as a major trading complex in the later Iron Age. However, it is worth keeping sites like Sudbrook Camp in mind. This large, and now heavily eroded, promontory fort near to Caerwent, with still hugely impressive multivallate defences surviving on its inland side, was well placed to act as a port. Perhaps in the later Iron Age such larger coastal sites replaced or supplemented the more ad hoc creek ports. It's certainly an idea worth considering.

There is another factor that we should also consider. Unlike some Iron Age tribal communities, the Silures did not, at least as far as we know, produce coins. However, sufficient numbers of coins minted in other regions have been found in the Silurian region to confirm that they were well enough aware of them.

Coins of other British polities like the Durotroges and the Trinovantes have been found, as well as two Gallic coins, one of them coming from the Turones, a tribe based in the Loire region of what is today France. The large majority of coins found in the Silurian region, however, were Dobunnic issues. The Dobunni were the tribe centred on modern Gloucestershire. We have already encountered these close neighbours of the Silures in our discussion of Caratacus.

While the majority of Dobunnic coins have unsurprisingly been found in the east of the Silurian region, there have been examples found over a wide area; find sites include Caldicot, Chepstow, Dingestow, Llanthony, St Arvans, Tintern, Trelech and Whitton.

It is probably important that, unlike in the Dobunnic region itself, a high per-centage of these coins are gold. A good assumption seems to be that they were not being used as currency in any conventional sense. Perhaps it was just a convenient way to 'store' wealth. Arguably the most important thing about these coins is the simple fact that they were being used for something and they are a good indicator of trade and exchange.

There is another particularly interesting coin find; this one was a silver coin found near Penrhyndeudraeth. What makes it especially important is that it is inscribed 'CARA' – clearly suggesting that this is a coin of Caratacus himself.

The distribution of coins strengthens the argument for effective trade networks to and within Siluria. This section on trade has been speculative in many respects. If I were trying to write this in a more academic way, I might prefer the term theoretical. Theory in archaeology is good. However, as I explained at the outset, I'm not doing that, so I'm happy enough with speculative. Though it is at least, I hope, informed speculation.

In the chapter I've suggested boats as well as coastal and riverine movement of goods, despite not actually having an Iron Age boat to show you. But as you have seen, there are bits of Bronze Age boats and a good example of a Romano-Celtic vessel. In addition, we have trade goods from far enough afield to make water transport seem the most likely way to have moved them. Given that the Mendip ceramics found at Llanmelin came from south of the Bristol Channel, I find it hard to visualise them being moved any way other than by boat from somewhere like Portishead to a convenient landing place like Sudbrook straight across the Channel.

Moreover, with sites like Llanmaes there are good candidates for coastal entre-pots even in the earlier Iron Age. Add all this up and while there is still an element of speculation, overall it looks a pretty safe bet to me. Consequently, I think that we can safely say that we are dealing in well-informed speculation, which is no bad thing.

As we're being speculative, let's end this chapter on an arguably even more speculative note. I was taken by an idea put forward in a book called *Prehistoric Wales* published back in the year 2000. In discussing two small, early Roman forts on the north Devon coast at Old Burrow and Martinhoe, the authors discuss why they might have been constructed. Their suggestion is that they could have been 'designed to ward off seaborne raids by the still unconquered Silures'.

Now there's an idea to mull over! I find it hard, hand on heart, to think that the Silures were particularly likely to have been mounting cross-Bristol Channel raids on the Roman coast of Devon. But if the Romans believed that they might have done, that would speak volumes about the way they perceived their opponents in the Silurian War.

5

Commerce:
The daily grind

Whatever the impact of trade on the people of the Silurian region, it seems likely that daily life was largely concerned with local and immediate issues like food production. It is true that there is evidence for some industrial processes.

As we have already seen, there is good evidence for metalworking in the region with, among other things, apparently regional styles suggesting local production of objects like harness mounts. In addition to possible regional variation in some bronze items, there is also good evidence of ironworking on a number of sites. I can personally attest to some of them.

Slag is the distinctive waste product from ironworking with readily recognisable smithing slags, frequently accompanied by hammer scale created by the hammering of the hot iron, and the generally heavier smelting slags from primary production. Through the years, I've worked on many ironworking sites – heavy slag deposits can make excavating with a trowel more than a little bit difficult!

That's why I unwisely tempted fate on Lodge Hill one day. Morning coffee break under the trees was always a nice pause in the day's routine during the time we were working there. I remember well one morning musing about how it was a pleasant change not to be digging in slag. Coffee break ended and we returned to work – I think it took less than five minutes before the first slag was found!

In the event, this was a good thing. Confirmation of *in situ* ironworking, in this case smithing, added an important piece to the hillfort jigsaw. It was awkward stuff to work on but we really were quite pleased to see it.

Other artefacts help us to come closer to a somewhat ephemeral aspect of the Silurian system, albeit one that was probably absolutely central to society. We've already seen that sickles formed a part of the important early assemblage found at Llyn Fawr. Other finds from sites like the Twyn y Gaer and Llanmelin hillforts include querns. In the region, saddle querns tend to be early while more efficient rotary querns developed later to replace them. Sickles, of course, were for harvesting and most of us tend to think first of grain. This fits well with the querns, which were for grinding grain. Together they suggest arable farm production.

Those familiar with modern farming in south Wales might tend to expect something else as well. Grazing is important today, with a lot of sheep in the countryside. It seems reasonable to expect them to have been pretty important in the Iron Age as well.

Unfortunately, pastoral farming is frequently difficult to demonstrate artefactually. There are, however, types of durable objects that provide pretty persuasive clues. Textiles tend to perish, as do things associated with their production like wooden looms. Happily, a few things survive and items like loom weights and spindle whorls provide a snapshot of wool use.

Of course, pastoral economies do more than shear sheep. Meat production is a key consideration but, with notable exceptions such as Llanmaes and its predominance of butchered pig bone, evidence is sometimes more difficult to find.

What we do have are bone assemblages in excavation reports. You might find going through these in detail a bit tedious but it is interesting that they include a not surprising range of assemblages that frequently include bones from cattle, sheep and pigs, with cattle and sheep tending to dominate.

Excavations at Llanmaes provided good evidence of feasting, probably associated with trade. Trade must have been a key factor in the Iron Age economy. (National Museum of Wales)

Other bones are sometimes found including presumably non-domestic species like red deer. Perhaps unsurprisingly, given what we've already considered, horse bone is also sometimes found. It's worth noting that, especially on upland sites with acidic soil, bone survival may be limited; on Lodge Hill, for example, the only surviving bones that could be identified came from sheep and chicken. I suspect that is telling us more about soil conditions than it is about lifestyle.

By and large, the predominance of cattle and sheep almost certainly provides us with useful insight into the working of the rural economy. Other types of evidence may also be telling us about the importance of animals like cattle. A copper alloy bull's head mount from Chepstow could be a case in point. One of the most telling signs, however, is probably not bone or artistic representations. As in many good detective stories, footprints may be one of our best clues. Hundreds of cattle footprints closely associated with Iron Age structures at Goldcliff, for example, provide graphic confirmation of cattle management there.

What we presently lack in south-east Wales is detailed, comparative bone studies like those conducted in a few other parts of Britain. Studies in the Upper Thames Valley and in Wessex, for example, have resulted in better understanding of matters like the balance between cattle and sheep in those regions. Studies of age, butchery marks, etc. point to large-scale beef production in some areas.

The level of detail provided by these studies from southern England would be welcome in south-east Wales and would clarify the nature of the pastoral rural landscape more fully. No doubt such studies will come in due course. In the meanwhile, however, the evidence that we have allows us a degree of confidence in assuming the Silures to have had a mixed agricultural economy with pastoral production being pivotal.

Up and down: Back and forth?

Those cattle footprints from Goldcliff may tell us more than that there were once many cattle in and around the buildings. They may also be saying something about grazing practices in the Silurian region.

There is good medieval evidence, both early and late, that Wales was in part a transhumant society in the Middle Ages. Transhumance is the practice of people moving with their stock from usually low-lying farmsteads and associated fields to summer pastures in upland areas. This transitory system is still practised in some parts of Europe, like the Pyrenees, today. A graphic indication of this seasonal mobility, not so very long ago in Wales, is found in numerous place names throughout the country.

There are many Welsh hendref and hafod place names. Hendref was the name given to the old or main farm in the lowlands, while shelter on upper summer pastures was provided by the hafod, the summer house. You only have to look at a modern map and start counting hafod and hendref place names to find evidence of a transhumant past!

Goldcliff, however, seems to be suggesting an important variation in the theme. It looks likely that, in low-lying areas near the sea, summer pasture was less a case of moving up and more one of 'down and out'. The cattle once milling about around the Goldcliff structures were probably there because in the drier summer months fresh grazing was provided on the Levels.

As we look inland, the landscape becomes hillier, and ultimately we are presented with mountains. In these non-coastal areas the more common and arguably more traditional upland pastures seem to have been preferred.

Indeed, some earthworks associated with hillforts and other smaller enclosed upland sites are best explained as livestock management features. Cases in point include Glamorgan hillforts like Gaer Fawr (there are other similarly named sites like Gaer Fawr in Gwent, which isn't surprising as the name simply means 'big fort') and Y Bwlwarcau, where space within the concentric main earthworks suggests drove ways.

Clearly, we would be delighted to have more evidence on farming practices and detailed bone studies such as those having been undertaken in parts of England could be particularly helpful in improving our understanding of the pastoral economy. However, the evidence currently in hand does point to a mixed agricultural system, with grazing being an important element. Moreover, a case can be made for a transhumant system with movement of pastoralists and their flocks/herds from winter to summer pastures.

When we combine evidence of an agricultural economy supplemented with other activities such as metalworking and stimulated by trade, we begin to come closer, I believe, to understanding the lifestyle of the Silures before the Roman invasion.

Perhaps it's best to leave it at that for the moment and to turn our attention to other aspects of life in Siluria. It's about time to make a 'house call' or two – let's try to meet the Silures at home.

6

The Silures at home: Life in the round

There is an important point to be made here at the outset of our discussion of this topic – the Silures lived in roundhouses. This really is worth stressing. It is obvious that we are far, far from having seen anything like a diagnostic cross-section of domestic structures in the region. However, those that we have suggest that the Silures, like other peoples of Iron Age Britain, lived in roundhouses. And that was a matter of choice.

Roundhouses appear to have become ubiquitous in Britain by the late Bronze Age. That matter of choice that I have just referred to is possibly suggested by the excavation at Lodge Hill. There we explored post holes apparently indicating at least two buildings. One was a rectangular post-built structure with no obvious evidence of occupation. Eight post holes enclosing a paved area defined a small (7.2 x 9.8ft / 2.2 x 3m) rectilinear building.

We've already discussed the difficult soil conditions on the site and these make interpretation difficult in many areas. At least one post pairing, however, might be interpreted as an entrance for a larger, presumably domestic, circular structure. The case could not be made unequivocally but if this is the proper interpretation it fits in well with the broader picture that is emerging in the region.

I don't intend to try to provide anything like a gazetteer of known roundhouses from the area here as it is difficult to be exhaustive and hopefully the list will continue to grow rapidly. However, excavation and/or good geophysical survey results have indicated roundhouses at sites including Barry Holmes, Bishopston Valley, Cae Summerhouse, Caerau, Castle Ditches, Coed y Bwnydd, Coed y Caerau, Dunraven Castle, Harding Down, High Pennard, Hygga, Llanmaes, Llanmartin, Nash Point and Sudbrook Camp. We can, at the very least, say that roundhouse occupation was widespread in the Silurian region.

But what about the little rectangular structure on Lodge Hill, you may be asking? It isn't alone. Thanks to the important long-term investigations undertaken by Martin Bell and his team, our best-understood regional Iron Age landscape in south-east Wales is on the Levels. This hugely difficult tidal area, subject to daily flooding with all the associated silt deposits, has produced remarkable preservation.

In addition to a complex network of brushwood trackways, several rectangular structures have been found in this intertidal zone with good examples of groups of buildings from near Magor and around Goldcliff Point. These were large, the largest nearly 20 x 26 ft (6 x 8m). These structures include those surrounded by all of those cattle tracks that we talked about earlier.

There's a clue here, I think. As far as we can tell, all of these rectangular buildings were, like the little structure on Lodge Hill, ancillary. On the other hand, the round buildings were where people were living.

There is a danger that we might be inclined to go with the once fashionable idea that Iron Age populations lived 'in the round' and were only introduced to rectangular buildings when the Romans started to build them after the conquest. If you were inclined to think that, it's probably best to think again. It's clear that the Silures, like other British Iron Age communities, knew how to and indeed did build rectangular buildings. However, they used them as barns, byres, storage sheds, etc. They chose to live in roundhouses, and that must be telling us something.

The view from the roundhouse

A preference for living in roundhouses raises all sorts of interesting questions about the thought processes of the people who were living in them. Plenty of possible explanations have been offered.

In recent years, a number of studies have wrestled with the question, with some offering a range of cosmological explanations while others have leaned toward alternative answers as varied as identifiable differential use of space, gender-driven considerations and other symbolic issues.

If your head is reeling from the implications of some of these explanations, don't worry. I've decided the matter is too complex, and perhaps too theoretical, for a book like this. Suffice to say that I've seen, indeed supervised and examined, some very interesting theses on the subject. All have been instructive – particularly what I thought was a very incisive analysis of the use of space in early medieval Irish roundhouses. I'll point you at some of these in the notes. However, for now, let's concentrate on possibly more mundane issues like building them and their daily use.

There are well-known and particularly interesting examples of reconstructed, or perhaps more accurately 'constructed', groups of roundhouses. Examples include the famous Butser Farm in Hampshire on the South Downs of England. Others are at the National Museum of History, to many still the Welsh Folk Museum, at St Fagans where the original 'Celtic Village' has given way to the Bryn Eryr buildings.

Both Bryn Eryr and Butser are examples of trying to construct buildings carefully based on plans derived from archaeological evidence. In other words, place the hearth where excavation has demonstrated burning, put posts where post holes have been found, etc.

An excellent example where the process is being carried out *in situ*, i.e. buildings built on the excavated site itself, with features literally placed where they were found is Castell Henllys near Eglwyswrw in west Wales.

With my son David, I've also had a go at building a couple of roundhouses on Brynheulog, the smallholding where I live; he has subsequently built more including projects with his own students. It's an interesting activity that helps us to understand how these buildings might have been built and used.

There's a really important caveat here. We're learning how roundhouses *could* have been built and how they *might* have been used. Remember that we have only the archaeological evidence, usually simply a ground plan of post holes, a hearth, possible working surfaces and artefact spreads. We don't have any first-hand accounts nor do we have any sort of plans above ground level.

The large Brynheulog roundhouse. Building these structures at least gives us a good idea how they might have been built in the Iron Age. Look closely and you will see that the 'window' is closed! (Ray Howell)

For example, can you build an internal platform, in effect giving you a loft? It's done in some roundhouses; there are contemporary examples from around the world where it is. Clearly, then, the answer is that you can – but that doesn't mean that they did. There are villages in Papua today that do. That fact doesn't mean that it was done in Iron Age Wales and we don't often have evidence one way or the other. Even likely looking stake holes can't really make the case convincingly.

This was graphically brought home to me as we began to thatch our second roundhouse, a big one, at Brynheulog. David said, 'There's a good view this way – we ought to put in a window.' My instinctive reaction, as you can probably guess, was 'Iron Age roundhouses didn't have windows!' I stopped short immediately, remembering the advice I've just given you. We only have a ground plan. With respect to a window, I realised that we don't actually know whether they did or not.

In the end, it was a good view – the Black Mountains on the horizon. Consequently, we added a window. I thought it was a quite inventive solution. We made a hinged flap that could be propped open or, when it rained, pulled down, becoming just another bit of thatch. I'm not pitching the idea that the Silures had loads of windows in their buildings – just pointing out that they could have done.

Resilient reeds (or something)

There were two Brynheulog roundhouses. One was a small 'Let's try to sort out how to do this' kind of roundhouse, which we built on one of the few flat areas up a steep slope in the woods. Neighbours described it as a two-man roundhouse. Truth be told, it was more of a one man and a dog roundhouse!

The second was a much larger affair with an inner ring of posts built on a 'made' platform in our largest field. We thatched both with bracken. I know that we assume that the favoured thatching material was, as it still is, reed and no doubt it works well. However, we don't have much reed on Brynheulog – there's a bit of artistic license there. We don't have any reed on Brynheulog!

What we do have in abundance is bracken, and it is surprising how well it works. This probably explains why cottages were thatched with bracken in some places, including parts of Scotland, as late as the nineteenth century. What you have to do is tie the bracken into bundles (use your imagination and assess your bracken; seven to twelve stalks seems to work pretty well). The bundles are then tied tightly together to make an effective thatch.

I think the lesson here is that we are dealing with vernacular architecture. You use what is available. It probably isn't a coincidence that in parts of Britain some Iron Age sites have considerable quantities of bracken spores, etc.

The reed beds below us on the Levels probably would have produced excellent and arguably more 'traditional' thatching material. We weren't inclined to go down and cut it, never mind then hauling it to and then up the slope at Brynheulog. Neither was I going to buy it in. So, we went with what we had to hand and it worked well. I'll bet the Silures would have done the same.

As far as use of the buildings go, I'm not sure our approach would gain much approval as experimental archaeology. I found the roundhouses great places to go for a bit of quiet reflection and David had some successful student parties there. I don't suppose either activity tells us much about life in the Iron Age.

What I can tell you about our roundhouses is that they were dry, even in a Welsh winter, and, with the fire in, warm and comfortable. They were also remarkably strong. The little house in the woods was built under a very large, mature ash. One night in a storm a large branch broke and was blown right on top of the round-house – it simply bounced off! No damage done.

This doesn't bring us any closer to explaining a preference for roundhouses over rectangular ones. No doubt there are pros and cons to both. I once gave a lecture in the then recently completed Bryn Eryr structure(s) – at St Fagans a double roundhouse has a connecting passage between the two – pay a visit; you'll see what I mean.

There was a good turnout. Indeed, there was a full house at Bryn Eryr. I like to use PowerPoint simply for images. We immediately found a problem with a round building – if you put up a screen and fill the roundhouse a significant part of your audience can't see the screen properly. We managed. Besides, I'm pretty sure that the Silures didn't have much use for PowerPoint. It was, however, a graphic demonstration of just one difference between a round and a rectangular space. I am sure that there are many other more relevant ones.

Perhaps we should leave it there for now. It's probably time to move on to discuss, and to try to understand, the location of many of the excavated roundhouses that have been found. Many were found in the hillforts that dot the landscape throughout the region.

There's just one thought before we move on, though. Much has been written about the orientation of roundhouses. This is an area of study that has led to many of the cosmological explanations for roundhouse construction that we considered briefly before. I imagine that a range of motivations, some perhaps quasi-religious, could have been factors. However, practical matters must also have been important.

When we were building our roundhouses, our two main considerations with respect to orientation, i.e. basically where to put the door, were the lie of the land and the direction of the prevailing wind. Both considerations are quite important and must be incorporated into your planning from the outset. I feel confident that Iron Age communities would have been acutely aware of both issues and that they would have taken them fully into account before any round-house construction began.

7

The hills were alive

The most obvious Iron Age landscape features of south-east Wales, as with many parts of Britain, are the prominent, usually elevated and enclosed, sites commonly called hillforts. Their less common but clearly important and almost certainly related counterparts are the promontory forts, enclosed sites at a number of coastal locations.

We see immediately the need for different nomenclature to describe these sites. The coastal locations are not compatible with the description hillfort for the very good reason that they tend not to be on hills. However, as we have already seen, there is tension with the term hillfort itself.

As we've discussed with respect to the term chariot, some members of a generation of archaeologists who succeeded their post-war predecessors were uncomfortable with the martial tone of the hillfort description. They pointed out, no doubt correctly, that these enclosed sites could have had a range of functions that had nothing to do with conflict or defence. They could have been trading centres, repositories for surplus production, stock enclosures, religious sites, expressions of prestige, status symbols, ways to mobilise collective resources or statements of identity.

I have to say that I have never seen much tension between these various possibilities. The sites we tend to call hillforts could have been any of these things. Indeed, they could have been all of them. None of the suggestions seem mutually exclusive to me.

In addition to this, these sites would not necessarily have had a single purpose at any one time or the same purpose throughout their period of occupation. As we will see, the limited excavation that has taken place indicates that most were occupied over centuries. A prime function at one point could well have given way to another a hundred years or more later.

What does seem apparent, at least to me, is that in some regions we begin to see these enclosed, elevated sites emerging in the late Bronze Age, a time when there is a body of evidence suggesting social change, possibly accelerated by climate change, and consequent increasing competition for resources with associated tensions.

Moreover, while a site surrounded by large earth and or stone banks, often with stone revetment, may well be a powerful status symbol demonstrating a particular regional identity, it is also a site that can be defended. Whether or not they were primarily built as defensive structures, they were clearly defendable.

Given what we already know about the Silures, I think that, particularly in their region, we should stick with the 'tried and tested' definition. I'm describing these sites as hillforts and suggest that you do the same.

This is not an idle academic debate. These sites are important. As the dominant features in our landscape that survive from the Iron Age, we need to understand them as well as possible if we are to have any chance of better understanding the Iron Age peoples who built and used them.

Digging deeper (or just more)

As we've seen, hillforts were the most obvious Iron Age landscape features and there were lots of them. In order to understand them better, we need to investigate as many as we can. Unfortunately, at the time of writing, we've still barely scratched the surface.

I made this point in the first Silures book. Indeed, I think a few critics thought I over-egged the need to dig hillforts. Personally, I don't think so. I thought it was a critical point in that first book and I haven't changed my mind. I said it then – I intend to say it again here. (You can't make a key point too often, I hope.)

We need more investigation of these sites throughout south-east Wales, particularly as there seems to be some evidence, inevitably limited, of regional differences indicating at least a measure of variation from place to place. Multiple uses seem likely. The Caerau excavation will improve the picture in Glamorgan but there are many more upland sites there that are crying out for attention.

Much of my own work has focused on Gwent and I have to tell you that there is a big 'Gwent Gap'. This is not a gap in hillforts, although there is an interesting 'empty' area to consider. The gap I'm referring to is the gap in hillfort investigations, which is huge.

For information, I'm using Gwent as a geographical indicator because, for reasons that will become apparent, it is a long-standing and useful description with particular reference to the subject that we are considering. It is also a description with fewer complicating modern connotations than any obvious alternatives. I could have explained this in the end of chapter notes. I thought it was probably important enough to address in the text.

Gazetteers have been compiled with lists of hillforts in Gwent; worryingly, there are a number of variations within them. What seems safe to say is that there were more than fifty enclosed upland sites in Gwent that can confidently be described as hillforts.

As I pointed out in the first book, when we completed our work on Lodge Hill, it represented only the fifth of these sites to have had any investigation by excavation at all. That seemed shocking to me. Unfortunately, over a decade later nothing has changed. It remains only one of five, out of more than fifty, to have had serious archaeological investigation and one of those is now actually in Powys. If that sounds like a poor record and this information is new to you, hold on to your hat — it's actually far worse than it sounds.

Our work on Lodge Hill was limited. It was an excavation funded as a millennium project by the Charles Williams Educational Trust and was always intended to be a comparatively small and targeted initial exploration of what is a large hillfort site. In the end, we were very pleased with some quite important findings from limited sampling. The importance of these findings, remember we have already discussed the pottery assemblage including the important briquetage, simply demonstrate how even limited excavation can tell us a lot. A little excavation goes a long way! But, by the same token, no excavation at all doesn't.

Of the other four 'Gwentian' sites, there have been two post-war excavations. 'Post-war' sounds an increasingly anachronistic description so let's put it another way. In the past seventy-five years, only three hillforts have been explored by excavation. The other two were local group initiatives that included investigations by the Abergavenny Archaeology Group under the direction of Allan Probert on Twyn y Gaer and work on Coed y Bwnydd directed by Adrian Babbidge then of Pontypool Museum.

Results at Coed y Bwnydd were summarised in a twenty-page report in the *Monmouthshire Antiquary* published in 1977. The only summary of the work on Twyn y Gaer is a chapter in a National Museum publication called *Welsh Antiquity* published in 1976. I was later acquainted with both excavators. Shortly before his death, Allan confided in me his concern that a full report on Twyn y Gaer had still not been produced. Sadly, it never was.

The other two excavations were large-scale investigations directed by Victor Nash-Williams of the National Museum of Wales. The sites chosen were the tantalisingly complex appearing Llanmelin, on high ground approximately a mile north of Caerwent, and the impressive if highly eroded coastal promontory fort at Sudbrook south of the former civitas capital. Llanmelin was published in 1933; Sudbrook in 1939. Let's state the obvious: the results of both these excavations were published over eighty years ago.

Inevitably, there are problems with excavations conducted in the 1930s. Nash-Williams meticulously investigated these sites according to the normal practice of the time but it was a long time ago and accepted approaches have changed dramatically.

One major problem arises from the narrow trenching strategy adopted. If you want to get a feel for just how narrow the trenches were, go up and have a look. There are one or two that weren't back-filled to modern standards. Watch where you step.

Working in narrow trenches as opposed to current 'open-area' approaches inevitably leads to a very restricted understanding of what is going on at a site. Recent geophysical survey at Llanmelin, undertaken by Daryl Williams and others, has revealed among other things a number of clearly defined roundhouses. One of Nash-Williams's narrow trenches went right through the middle of one of them!

If you read his notes in the National Museum, you can see that he and his team recognised that there was a change of some sort. There were both colour and texture changes in the house but the narrow view that they had in their trench was not enough to allow them to understand what had caused the changes. This is not a criticism of the excavator or of his team, who were doing exactly what the textbooks of the time said they ought to do. The quality of the work that they did is seen in the amount of information they were able to extract and publish.

However, they were shackled by the conventions of the time. If we ask what did we really learn about life in the interior of the hillfort, it is hard to reach any conclusion apart from 'not much'. We certainly didn't learn anything like what we would expect to know after a major modern open-area excavation.

Happily, Cadw and the Glamorgan-Gwent Archaeological Trust have had occasion to revisit both sites more recently and conduct some targeted excavation, reopening some of Nash-Williams's trenches and conducting geophysical surveys. These new investigations are very welcome. They cannot, however, provide the sort of open-area excavations that may provide the explanations we ultimately need.

I suggested when we began this brief overview that we had just scratched the surface when it comes to the hillforts of south-east Wales. That can be seen as, at best, an understatement. So before moving on, I'll leap on my hobby horse once again: we need a great deal more investigation, including large-scale open-area excavations on the hillforts of the region.

At this point, I suspect some would recommend a throwing up of hands and a reluctance to proceed on the basis that when it comes to hillforts in the Silurian region, we haven't got a clue. Don't take that view. We do know some things and can, I think, infer some others.

There's a useful Welsh expression that is sometimes used when someone is exasperated and ready to throw in the towel, a sort of 'let's just go down to the pub' idiom. It's *rhoi'r ffidil yn y tô* – put the fiddle in the roof (loft might be a better translation). Let's not do that.

A good starting point is probably to see what can be gleaned from the hillfort excavations that have taken place and see how we might tease out a bit more. Keep the fiddle ready and let's go through them.

What have we learned?

As I mentioned, one thing that the narrow trenching techniques of the 1930s could be reasonably good at is helping us to understand construction sequences of ramparts. With luck and good sampling, we might also hope to gain some dating sequences. Nash-Williams thought that sequences at Llanmelin might have been roughly 200 BC to AD 75; he suggested that construction phases at Sudbrook could have been second century BC with occupation well into the Romano-British period. For several reasons, it is probably worth re-examining this date range more carefully.

A radiocarbon date led Probert to suggest a fifth-century BC start date for Twyn y Gaer. Coed y Bwnydd, it is suggested, was early to middle Iron Age with radio-carbon dates for one roundhouse put at *c.* 550–350 BC. Babbidge reported little evidence of activity later than the third century BC.

These dates are potentially quite significant because they emphasise one of the problems with Welsh hillfort studies, one that we will have to consider carefully later. On the basis of these suggested construction dates, it is possible that a site like Coed y Bwnydd was abandoned before construction on the promontory fort at Sudbrook began.

The obvious problem is that we don't know which of these sites were contempo-rary and that presents big problems when we start to look at the spatial relationships between hillforts, which is precisely what I intend to suggest to you in the final chapter.

There is a not dissimilar variation in suggested dates for Glamorgan sites that have been investigated. For example, a construction date as late as the second century BC has been suggested for the Castle Ditches site near Llancarfan. On the other hand, dates of *c.* 700 BC were obtained at Coed y Cymdda near Dinas Powys. As we have already seen, early results from Caerau near Ely, where meticulous ongoing work is continuing, show very early activity on that site.

One of the benefits that we would hope to derive from further excavations is a better understanding of construction dates, building sequences, etc. As I men-tioned in Chapter 2, relying on one historical source is uncomfortable. So is trying to date phases of a hillfort from one or two radiocarbon dates, especially if the samples were taken half a century ago.

With historical sources, there's not much we can do about only having one – we're unlikely to find another Tacitus. With an excavation programme, however, there is every chance of building up a good body of dates derived from careful sampling at a number of sites.

One of the things that we can compare relatively easily is ramparts. Virtually all will have been eroded and only a few have had excavation trenches dug into them. By and large, however, with notable exceptions like part of the circuit at Sudbrook that has fallen into the sea, the ramparts are still there. Consequently, we might start by counting them.

Vallation simply describes the number of banks and ditches enclosing a site. Sites can be univallate, with one bank and associated ditch, bivallate with two, or multivallate with several, i.e. more than two.

It has been suggested that some hillforts like Llanmelin may have begun as univallate sites with a 'structured' bank, then subsequently developed into multivallate ones with glacis or sloping defences. These were frequently revetted, i.e. faced with masonry or in the case of hillforts, stone. What this means is open to interpretation.

Were multivallate sites more important, was there a greater perceived threat, a stronger desire to make a statement? We can't be sure but, at the very least, vallation gives us an easy starting point for comparison. Of course, location must have been critical. Twm Barlwm, which dominates so much of south-east Wales, for example, is a univallate site. However, in its position it's hard to see why you would

Defences at Sudbrook, a promontory fort which gives us a classic example of vallation. Notice the triple banks and separating ditches. The 'new Severn Bridge' in the background is a useful reminder of the site's proximity to the sea, making Sudbrook an ideal port location. This photo is taken from a cement-built Second World War structure constructed on the large inner rampart, saying something else about its continuing strategic location. (Ray Howell)

for any reason feel a need for additional banks. On the other hand, given the steep approaches, it's easy to see why you wouldn't want to try to build any.

As I've been arguing, excavation can clarify interpretation of earthworks. An interesting case in point is Twyn y Gaer, where crossbanks seem to subdivide the hillfort, creating three inner enclosures. A question that comes to mind is whether this might be telling us that the site was expanded or reduced in size at some time. After excavation, Probert became convinced it was the latter. He even suggested that a reduction in the enclosed area brought the site closer in form to that of hill-forts to the south. His idea was that this might represent expansion by the Silures, north into Powys.

Recent geophysical survey appears to indicate a now lost bank at Llanmelin, that would suggest that at this site there was expansion, not contraction. The annex at Llanmelin was a late addition but this and the associated enclosures are enigmatic and probably easier to consider in the next chapter.

The most recent research excavation, by about thirty years, is our investigation at Lodge Hill. With a limited initial scope, very challenging soil conditions and extensive tree root damage, interpretation of the site was difficult. Josh Pollard in particular worked at length to make sense of it all. Here are what we think some of the findings indicate.

It's best to begin with a brief explanation of the site. Lodge Hill is large, over 1,300 x 650ft (400 x 200m). It is emphatically multivallate with, in places, an impressive triple bank enclosure that at one point in its circuit spreads to no fewer than five lines of bank and ditch. Today there is a small entrance on the western end of the site and there was almost certainly a second, larger, main entrance on the south-east now obscured by buildings and groundworks of Lodge Farm.

Of particular interest was an inner enclosure to the south, which is where we decided to concentrate our efforts. Given restraints of time and resources we opened three main areas associated with the inner enclosure. One was an area of nearly 350ft (106 m) in the interior; the second was a 6ft 6in (2m) wide trench that extended for nearly 70ft (21m) across the inner bank and ditch; and a third was a nearly 100ft (30m) investigation of the entrance and associated passageway.

The results have been fully published and, as previously, I'll point you to the excavation report and related bibliographical material in the chapter notes. Here, let's just summarise some of the highlights.

We've already discussed the La Tène brooch and talked about pottery with the bri-quetage, which seems to be showing us riverborne trade. What we haven't discussed is the late Roman pottery, which indicates reoccupation of the hillfort. That is arguably one of the most exciting discoveries and we'll come back to it in due course.

The entrance also proved to be very interesting. We were able to describe a sequence that is fascinating and could hardly have been hinted at without exca-vation. The first phase entrance with an apparently associated 'guard chamber' probably dates from the hillfort's inception. Subsequently, however, the entrance was blocked and filled in completely. At some later date, which unfortunately couldn't be determined, it was cut through and reinstated. This alone would justify going back to the site for further investigation.

Excavation of the inner bank and ditch also proved instructive. The steep slope here made excavation challenging in a trench that came to be known affection-ately as 'Chad's ski slope'; the work was supervised by Adrian Chadwick. Among the indications here was not only that there had been revetment, but also collapse deposits that could suggest slighting. The Romano-British tile fragment recovered might be a 'smoking gun' of sorts.

It's easy to imagine that when the Roman army began building its large fortress at Isca, the Roman name for Caerleon, which is just below the hillfort, the idea of an even potentially occupiable hillfort in close proximity was not a welcome one. Slighting defences could also have been seen as very useful exercise for the troops.

Add to this, the post placements and other evidence of structure, along with the ironworking surface in the interior excavation, and you can probably see that we were pretty pleased with the results of a relatively small excavation. I know I was.

So where does all of this leave us and what should come next? Just before we started work on Lodge Hill, I had the opportunity to examine a very good and ultimately successful PhD thesis with Barry Cunliffe as the other examiner. In the pre-viva examiners' meeting, I couldn't resist showing the plan of the site to 'Professor Iron Age', the doyen of British Iron Age studies. I was pleased with his apparent enthusiasm, if a little taken aback by the scale of what he was saying he would do on the site. The suggested '40m here and 50m there' was on a rather different scale than we were in a position to contemplate! However, as you would expect, he was absolutely right and to take things any further that is exactly what you would have to do. Very large open-area excavation would be the appropriate next step on Lodge Hill.

Which brings us back to where we started this chapter. I don't want to sound like a broken record, but one more time let me stress that we need more excava-tion of these south Wales hillforts. Given the current state of the universities, the financial position of museums and the difficulties facing the archaeological trusts, that is sadly unlikely to happen.

However, I think Lodge Hill clearly shows that when you excavate, a little investment can go a long way. So, fingers crossed. But in the meanwhile, is there any 'bargain basement' research we can productively do straight away? I think there probably is and I'll share some thoughts with you in the final chapter.

In the meanwhile, however, let's have a look at something else. If you think hillfort studies are challenging, just wait until we start to think about religion! And that's next on the agenda.

8

Belief:
A world of spirits?

Religion can be a difficult area for archaeologists – it's frequently hard to derive an understanding of belief systems from archaeological evidence. A standing joke on many excavations is 'If you don't understand it, it's ritual.' Well, sometimes it is and sometimes it isn't.

An entertaining and useful game to play with undergraduates is to think of a place; the lecture hall or classroom is usually a good one to start with. Imagine a disaster of major proportions leaving the chosen space abandoned and subject to the usual natural processes. Then imagine coming back to the site a few hundred years later. What might survive? How much insight into the use of the space might it give us?

Now, to really present a challenge, do the same with the local parish church. Archaeologically, what would survive? What could that evidence tell us about the use of the building? How close would we come to understanding the Christian practices that took place there? Almost invariably, the answer is 'Not very close at all.'

So, we are left with some very difficult issues of interpretation. As often as not, one of the most helpful things we can do is turn to written records of rites and practices that we think might be comparable. We start trying to compare by analogy. An inscription or two can sometimes also be very helpful.

In this particular case, an obvious place to begin is to read Roman descriptions of religious practices in other parts of Britain and to compare these with European examples contained in classical accounts. We try to make sense of our local examples against the backdrop of the wider study of 'Celtic religions'.

I don't know if you noticed, but we have just wandered into a minefield. Arguably, we should already have engaged with what might be described as the 'Celt debate'. We can't avoid it any longer. Are we actually dealing with Celtic religion? Indeed, are we even dealing with Celts?

Celticity and controversy

Were the people of Iron Age south-east Wales Celts? We certainly use the term freely today – we have had a 'Celtic League' in rugby, Celtic film festivals, Celtic music events. However, there are archaeologists who say we shouldn't, or at least that we should be sure not to use the description archaeologically.

The debate was begun with a bang by John Collis in an article that appeared in the journal *Studia Celtica* in 1996. It was then given a wider audience by Simon James in a British Museum book published in 1999. The basic argument is that classical writers never actually referred to the peoples of Britain as Celts, unlike some central and western European tribes that they did describe with the term (*Keltoi*). That's an oversimplification but it gives you a feel for what became a hot topic in archaeology. Indeed, many archaeologists began going to some lengths to avoid using the description.

It is true that taking material culture as an indicator of identity, ethnicity or political allegiances becomes a slippery slope almost immediately. Today, many people like to wear baseball caps. This doesn't make them Americans. Similarly, wearing a La Tène brooch or carrying a Hallstatt sword didn't necessarily make someone a Celt.

Long before the onset of the Celt debate, I had already formulated an answer to a not infrequently asked question. When asked if pre-conquest Wales was a Celtic society, my answer was always 'It depends on what you mean by Celtic.' I thought it should largely be a language descriptor. Let's see if that still holds true.

We had better begin by putting cards on the table. I have enjoyed having the opportunity to co-edit the first volume of the five-volume *Gwent County History* with my friend and colleague, and expert on Iron Age religion, Miranda Aldhouse-Green. We also co-authored a book for University of Wales Press in the year 2000. It was published in a new and updated edition by the same press in 2017. The title of the book was *Celtic Wales* – so you might have an inkling of which way I'm leaning on this one!

One of the very positive outcomes of the Celt debate was that it stimulated an even wider discussion. Of particular importance, I think, is a conference in Aberystwyth in 2008 organised by Barry Cunliffe and John Koch; it was followed by a second in Oxford. Both led to volumes titled *Celtic from the West,* with Volume 1 appearing in 2010 and Volume 2 in 2013. A third was published in 2016. Historical linguists, archaeologists and geneticists were brought together. Many challenged the orthodoxy of a 'Celtic Genesis' beginning in central and western Europe during the earliest Iron Age.

Instead, many took the idea of Celtic languages, a description coined by Edward Lhuyd in his *Archaeologia Britannica*, published in 1707. This family of related languages included not only modern variants of Gaelic and Brythonic languages such as Welsh, Irish, Cornish and Breton but, judging from fragments that have survived, also continental Gaulish. As our understanding has grown, the long pedigree of these languages has been clarified. Colin Renfrew, for example, suggests that both Welsh and Irish may have emerged as distinct languages as early as about 900 BC.

No doubt purists might argue that we should find a 'better' name for these languages but we've used Celtic languages as a descriptor for well over 300 years. It's hard not to think that trying to come up with an alternative would only confuse the issue.

What emerges in the volumes of *Celtic from the West* is a fascinating attempt to reconstruct 'proto Celtic', the 'common ancestor of all the attested Celtic languages'. Since the discovery of the first Celtiberian inscription in 1970, this search for roots has increasingly turned to the Iberian Peninsula; of particular interest is Tartessian, a language once spoken in what is today southern Portugal and south-west Spain. It is argued that Tartessian was a 'mature Celtic language' by the eighth century BC. This then leads to the idea that Celtic language may have originated in and spread from within the 'Atlantic zone' by the Bronze Age or even earlier, i.e. we have Celticisation from the west.

So where does this leave us? As I've told you, I've always tended to answer the 'Who and where were the Celts, and would we have found them in Wales?' questions with the observation that it depends on what you mean by Celt – if you mean use of an identifiable Celtic language, then the answer is yes.

I'm still happy with that. So, let's leave it there for now and move on to see what we can find out about the belief system of the Celtic-speaking Silures.

Spirits in the woods?

We've already seen that interpretation of evidence relating to belief systems can be difficult. The more limited our evidence is, the more difficult it becomes.

We know that pre-Iron Age religious sites abound in Britain. We all are familiar with such imposing places as Stonehenge and Avebury and their associated ritual landscapes. Trying to interpret exactly what they mean and how they were used is more problematic. Use as funerary monuments with veneration of ancestors is a popular interpretation at the moment. However, there are a number of alternatives and, I imagine, more to come.

Whatever the meanings of and ritual activities associated with these places, there are comparable sites in south-east Wales that seem to belong to the same tradition. Cases in point include the stone circle on Gray Hill and the standing stones at Trelech. Students and I joined colleague Mike Hamilton in his investigation of the latter. Geophysics had shown an offset sub-circular bank and ditch enclosure that, with excavation, proved to be Bronze Age in date.

Despite these sites, however, clearly Iron Age examples of foci for ritual activities are few and far between in the Silurian region. There's another of those understatements. In terms of confirmed ritual sites, if we are looking for some sort of megalithic successor to the henges or a proto temple complex, there aren't any.

It's true that aerial photographs have revealed field marks that could be consistent with a Romano-British temple at Gwehelog near Usk. This interpretation, as well as any pre-conquest activity there, however, can only be demonstrated by excavation.

One of the most exciting recent discoveries in south-east Wales is Toby Driver's 2018 aerial photographic coverage of sites on the Wyndcliff, which overlooks the river Wye not too far from Tintern. Recorded as part of the Royal Commission's ongoing aerial survey programme, these images show a villa in remarkable detail and an associated apparent enclosure that looks Iron Age in plan.

Both are relatively near the Gaer Fawr hillfort and, given the apparent complexity of the site plus the relatively close proximity of temple complexes like Lydney, some ritual associations must be among a number of possible interpretations. The site would surely repay further investigation by survey and ultimately excavation. We'll think a bit more about the potential of this landscape later.

For now, however, despite such recent discoveries from the air we are still apparently left with no obvious, confirmed Iron Age religious sites in our study area. That is unless we accept that we shouldn't be looking for buildings or defined enclosed spaces in the first place. Perhaps our starting point should be places like those where we have seen deposition of objects in 'watery contexts'.

It seems likely that locations like Llyn Fawr and Llyn Cerrig Bach were centres of continuing ritual activities. If we follow this line of thinking, we aren't necessarily looking for built features at all. This is probably not that surprising – to see why, let's do a bit of that comparison by analogy that we discussed previously.

Interestingly, and perhaps a little counterintuitively, one of our best accounts of what we've agreed to carry on calling Celtic religion comes from Julius Caesar. Caesar was particularly exercised by a priestly class that he identified as druids. The druids, he reported, were priests, philosopher-historians and judges, adjudicating on matters including tribal disputes. Their remit, which seems to have been in part a 'shamanistic' linking with a 'spirit world', was described as pan-tribal, with the druids able to pass freely even among warring groups.

This picture was fleshed out by other Roman observers like Pliny the Elder who, in his *Natural Histories*, described the symbolic significance of things like mistletoe, which he tells us was gathered by the druids with considerable ritual at appropriate times dictated by a lunar cycle. A persistent theme associated with these classical accounts of the druids was the importance of natural sites, the sacred groves that seem to have been central to their activities.

There is little doubt that the druids captured Roman imaginations. Classical observers generally appear to have been somewhere on a scale ranging from curious to horrified. The latter sentiment is frequently explained as a reaction to sacrificial rites. A key point, however, is that while the Romans were generally quite relaxed about the various religions that they encountered in their imperial expansion, there were certain things they would not accept.

Polytheistic themselves, the Romans were usually happy enough to reach some sort of accommodation with whatever local deities they encountered. They became concerned if they thought a belief system was overly secretive. The main exception, however, was any creed that challenged the imperial cult – that was perceived as a practice that threatened the empire itself. This aversion led at times to vicious suppression of groups like the early Christians and the followers of the druids.

We see that aversion translated into action after the Romans launched their invasion of Britain. It is clear that the realm of the druids included Britain and Ireland as well as Gaul. The Romans became convinced that much of the native opposition in Britain was down to the influence of the druids and consequently were determined to eradicate both them and their ideology. That's why, on the eve of the Boudican revolt, an event that may have had no small druidic input, much of the army was 'otherwise engaged'. It was busy attacking druids in Anglesey.

Once again, our source is Tacitus. As we have seen, the governor Quintus Veranius had attempted to resume hostilities against the Silures in AD 57, only to die shortly thereafter. In the following year, his successor Gaius Suetonius Paulinus went onto the offensive again. Instead of attacking the Silures, however, he struck into north Wales. His target was Anglesey, which he was convinced was the centre of British druidism. Tacitus gives us a graphic account of what followed. Suetonius, we are told, ordered construction of flat-bottomed boats for crossing the Menai Straits. Confronting the Roman army was a 'terrifying array', which included the druids themselves 'shouting dreadful curses'.

To complete the picture, this dense armed mass of people also included 'black-robed women with dishevelled hair like furies, brandishing torches'. We are told that, not for the first time in their campaign into Wales, the troops were 'paralysed with fear'.

However, Suetonius berated his men, telling them not to fear a 'horde of fanatical women'. In the event, the army crossed and, as was often the case in close-quarter fighting, defeated the defenders, who were 'engulfed in the flames of their own torches'. That wasn't all. He ordered his troops to destroy the sacred groves of Anglesey. This was a concerted effort to end native resistance with an attack on their religion and its priesthood. The destruction was aimed not at buildings or monuments but at the sacred forests that were at the heart of native ritual practice.

This, I think, is telling us something crucial about the Silures. They seem to have been, like other Iron Age communities throughout Britain and beyond, influenced by a religion derived from the natural world that surrounded them. Anglesey, presumably associated with the Ordovician heartland, was a centre of the druids. We know that the Silures and the Ordovices interacted. Remember that we think Caratacus was trying to combine the two at the beginning of the Roman invasion. The Ordovices were influenced by the druids; the same must have been true of the Silures.

There have even been interesting suggestions that some of the deposits of hoards from Silurian sites that we have discussed, like that at Seven Sisters, could have been a reaction to the Roman advance. Sacrifice of objects could take on important ritual significance at times of social stress. Indeed, it has also been suggested that 'Lindow Man', the bog body discovered in Cheshire, a victim of sacrifice, could have been a more extreme example of this same rite.

We have to be a bit careful at this point. It's easy, when we have little direct evidence, to devise belief systems that strike a chord with us today. These ideas might not actually have much to do with Iron Age religion. Modern druidism, for example, is an interesting area to study. Whether it derives much from the ideas of the druids in the Iron Age is another matter altogether.

However, there are important points for archaeologists to keep in mind including the fact that a lack of monuments or temples doesn't mean a lack of religious belief. Indeed, if the spirits were in the woods, there may be no trace of them at all. This doesn't mean that they were any less real for the people who believed in them.

Now I have to be careful. It sounds like I'm on the verge of pointing you toward a sort of quasi-Shinto for south Wales. I have no real insight into how they viewed 'the ancestors'. I don't really know if they found *kami*, spirits, in the woods. But it might not be such a bad working model.

There is another thing to factor into our modelling at this point and that is that in addition to grounding in the natural world there may also have been examples of anthropomorphism going on. Human characteristics were being assigned to deities or an assortment of other 'things'. As my colleague Miranda Aldhouse-Green has explained, 'personification of natural forces and their endowment with names often forms the foundation for polytheistic belief systems'. That might help put us on firmer ground.

Let's see if it helps us come closer to understanding belief systems among the Silures.

Ocelus and others

When we discussed historical sources, we ended that section by looking at inscriptions sometimes accompanying sculpted images. One of the examples was that of Ocelus, which you'll remember was mentioned in two important inscriptions from Caerwent, Venta Silurum. In one instance he was linked with Mars and Lenus, the Roman god and a Treverian deity from Gaul. In the other, there is a simple, direct linkage with Mars, the Roman god of war, who also often had a 'protective' role as well. Ocelus is also known, remember, from an inscription found in Carlisle where he was also linked with Mars. This may be quite important.

These inscriptions are obviously useful but they don't necessarily tell us much about pre-conquest practices. Celtic deities could have been borrowed from other areas after the social mixing that occurred in the aftermath of the conquest. The fact that Ocelus was also venerated at a northern British site doesn't necessarily change that. However, it just might strengthen the case for assuming that we are dealing with an 'indigenous' deity who was incorporated into the Roman pantheon.

It strengthens another assumption as well. The Silures, like other British Iron Age groups, seem to have been perfectly comfortable with the idea of multiple deities who could later be linked with Roman counterparts. This may give us more confidence in the view that anthropomorphic deities were already part of a Silurian pantheon before the conquest.

Other evidence seems to strengthen that supposition. One example, which appeals to me, seems to be steering us in that direction. I'll be candid with you; this idea is highly speculative and I could well be one of its few proponents. Still, I'll share it and you can see what you think. It isn't a new idea in the sense that I mentioned it in the first Silures book and George Boon had hinted at it even earlier. It is, however, one that doesn't have a queue of supporters so it is still not only speculative but also, I like to think, a bit innovative.

We will be discussing Caerleon, once the Roman fortress of Isca, in more detail in the next chapter. For now, I just want to think a bit about one feature found on some of their buildings, antefixa (Latin seems to have lost its 'gloss' these days and these are increasingly referred to as antefixes – more than one antefix anyway).

An antefix was a roof terminal, usually ceramic, which decorated and protected the join of the roof. It was protective not simply in terms of helping to keep out the elements but also, through its decorative motif, to ward off 'evil' that might threaten the building. At Caerleon, no fewer than seven of the antefixa that have been discovered feature a distinctive, presumably male, head. These are unusual in that the subject portrayed has obvious pointed ears, apparent fur and in several examples of pronounced whiskers.

At least one of these objects is usually on display in the main gallery of the National Roman Legion Museum in Caerleon, a branch of the National Museum of Wales. The remainder are carefully stored in the basement reserve collection. I've visited that basement with its stores many times, on a couple of occasions to look at each of these antefixa carefully. I'm struck by the cat-like appearance of the imagery. Indeed, with several examples, it's hard to interpret them as anything other than cats!

That's unusual. It's true that big cats like lions appear on some examples from farther afield. The Etruscans seem to have been fond of them early on. The British Museum has an antefix, found near Rome, with decoration portraying Artemis holding lions by their paws. These Caerleon 'cats', however, are different and seem to have imagery that, at least in detail, is unique to Caerleon. We have to wonder why?

We've discussed the widespread Roman practice of identifying, propitiating and, in some cases, appropriating local native deities. After a protracted and costly war with the Silures, it probably seemed like a good idea to get on the right side of any Silurian ones that you could identify.

I'm attracted by the idea of some sort of 'cat cult'. Let's be clear on this. I'm not thinking about domestic moggies! Keep in mind that there were wild cats in Wales, think lynx or something similar.

It's easy to imagine that a stealthy hunter of the forest like a lynx could be an appealing cult object for peoples like the Silures. It's equally easy to see why any such cult could seem an attractive one for troops who had been engaged in a guerrilla war in the woods against them for years.

There is even a possibility that a sort of folk memory might have survived into the medieval literature of the region and associated Celtic realms. An interesting example comes from Ireland, where the twelfth-century text *Còir Anmann* describes a hero, Cairbre Cinn-Cait (Cairbre of the Cat's Head), who had both the fur and ears of a cat!

From the heartland of the Silures, we have possibly even more direct references in medieval Welsh texts. In the Welsh triads, for example, there is a monster speckled cat called Palug. This ravenous beast is described as devouring 'nine score men for its food'. None of this, of course, proves the case. However, I think it's pretty persuasive. I'm sticking with this Silurian cat cult idea. If we do take this view, we find ourselves closer both to indigenous local spiritual traditions derived from the natural setting of the landscape of south-east Wales as well as anthropomorphism in local cult practice.

It may be speculative but it may also be a way of bringing us closer to an understanding of the belief system of the Silures.

Heads we win?

As we have just seen, interesting and unusual material from the Romano-British period may provide insights into belief systems of the Iron Age. There are some other examples that we should consider in this respect.

As we have already seen, and will discuss in more detail soon, Caerwent or Venta Silurum became the tribal capital of the Silures during the post-conquest or Romano-British period. Not surprisingly, a large number of Roman artefacts have been found in and around the town. However, other things have been excavated that seem to be hearkening back to the pre-conquest era.

A case in point is a stone statuette of a seated female figure, generally referred as a 'mother goddess', from Caerwent. She is wearing a hood and holding a fruit and a small fir, which can be seen as symbols of fertility and eternity. This figure is Roman in date but in inspiration seems to reflect, as Miranda put it in the *County History*, older 'local spirit-forces'.

The same may be true of the stone relief built into the wall of the Norman hall-keep at Chepstow castle. This is clearly a Roman relief in terms of its style and method, taken from a site nearby, possibly Caerwent. It fits in well with the regular layer of tegulae, Roman tiles, built into the hall-keep. The Normans were trying to make a political statement in Chepstow, identifying with the previous invading power in the region.

The imagery on the Chepstow example, however, is hardly classical. Three male figures, one much larger than the others, are portrayed with the large central figure apparently wearing some sort of animal headdress. Even without reference to the widespread 'triplism' of Celtic art, this appears to be a largely 'native' item.

Arguably the object that most graphically shows native tastes and traditions in and around Roman Caerwent is the starkly striking stone head found associated with a large courtyard house just inside the town's west gate.

It was recovered from a narrow room in a building set apart from the main house, numbered by excavators as House XI 7S. The head rested on a raised platform at one end of the narrow room. It is hard to interpret the platform as anything other than an altar. Carved from local sandstone, it is slightly less than 9in (22cm) in height.

The crafted sandstone image appears basic in its execution but elements such as the treatment of the eyes are consistent with Bronze and Iron Age examples from other parts of Britain as well as the continent and probably had ritual significance. Similar objects have been found at Carmarthen, Caerhun, Holt and on Steep Holm.

Martin Henig is widely regarded as one of Britain's leading experts on Roman art. I well remember a guest lecture that he gave to students on our MA course in

The 'mother goddess' from Caerwent, which seems to speak to us more of Silurian than Roman tradition. (National Museum of Wales)

The stone head from Caerwent, which wouldn't speak to us of Roman tradition at all – apart from the fact that it was venerated in the civitas capital very late in the history of Roman Britain. (National Museum of Wales)

Celto-Roman studies. One of the students asked him how much 'romanitas' was to be found in the Caerwent head. The answer was, 'absolutely none'!

It's important to remind ourselves that there was quite secure dating evidence found when the head was excavated. It was a fourth-century AD context. So, we have a purely native object being venerated in the civitas capital well over 300 years after the Silurian War. It seems clear that aspects of native tradition remained strong in the civitas capital, presumably the most Romanised bit of Siluria, even at the end of the Romano-British period. I think it's safe to say that it was a resilient tradition.

There may be other avenues open to explore the nature of that tradition. For example, there have been efforts to find vestigial Iron Age imagery in early medieval texts. As we have seen with the cat Palug and other references, this approach may pay dividends.

Another approach, and one of the commonest ways to try to understand belief systems, is by investigating funerary practice. This is an area where ritual often comes to the fore. However, it can be very difficult to do this for the British Iron Age. As has frequently been observed, for many parts of Britain, during various phases of the Iron Age, there is very little evidence that anyone ever died.

I've explored possibilities with students. Here's the question for today: what sort of funerary rite leaves no trace at all? Ruling out alien abduction, which was suggested a time or two, there are not many. Even in acid soils, you would expect some trace from any form of inhumation and might hope for some sort of ritual deposition in a 'watery context'. Cremation should leave pyres at least.

One practice, known historically from some parts of the world, which leaves little if any easily recoverable evidence, is excarnation or exposure. That's a possibility. At the end of the day, though, in most cases we just don't know.

There is, however, at least one tempting avenue that we could pursue. I told you that we would come back to the annex at Llanmelin. This addition to the hillfort is made up of three or four (it depends on how you want to count them) sub-rectangular enclosures. There is an associated bank and ditch along the south-east side of the annex.

These often used to be described as animal enclosures. I'm afraid that in one or two of the earliest things that I wrote referring to them I said this was a possibility. I suppose it is but I don't now think it's a very strong one.

I've subsequently been back up to have a closer look at them on many occasions. There's a pretty big problem; there are no obvious entrances. Unless you have exceptionally strong farmers, tossing their sheep over substantial ramparts, these aren't going to work very well as animal enclosures!

They do, however, look a lot like some late Iron Age cremation cemeteries in England. Possible parallels have been found at St Albans and Colchester. You have to wonder, given this similarity to excavated first-century BC and AD funerary sites, what was the significance of human remains found by Nash-Williams in the 1930s.

Two partial skeletons were found in his excavation of the enclosures and associated bank, one male and one female. These were associated with the two large enclosures in the annex. Could they have been part of a complicated funerary complex? There's really only one way that we might find out. You can't help thinking that a new, modern excavation addressing this possibility might reveal a great deal about this part of the hillfort. It's certainly worth a try — so here we are back where we've been several times before needing more excavation in hillforts. You can't really avoid that conclusion.

What you can conclude as well, I think, is that the limited and fragmentary evidence that we have seems to be suggesting a religious system among the Silures that was anchored in the natural world, influenced by druids and containing anthropomorphic deities and/or cult objects. I'm not sure that we can go much further at this stage. It's probably time to turn our attention to Roman south-east Wales.

What *did* they ever do for us?

Much has been written about Roman Wales. For our purposes here, the main concern is what impact the invasion and subsequent occupation of Silurian territory had on the indigenous population. Leaving aside psychological scars inevitably arising from a quarter-century-long war lost, important immediate effects must have included loss of land and a total transformation of trading networks.

An army of occupation would have begun to demand tribute and taxes. It would also have seized territory outright. The early fortress built at Usk, subject to frequent flooding and impossible to supply directly from the sea, gave way to Isca, today Caerleon (which appropriately translates as 'fortress of the legion').

There is good reason to think that the fertile Usk river valley between the two locations, several thousand hectares of prime fertile land, would have become the *territorium* of the legion, an area exploited directly by the army for raw materials as well as for pastoral and arable fields providing for the troops. The *territorium* probably extended even further. As we have already discussed, areas of the Levels may have become a *prata*, pastureland, for the army.

As far as trade is concerned, south-east Wales would have been rapidly incorporated into the Roman imperial system and a key early trading centre must have been the fortress itself. Less subject to flooding than Usk, tides flowing upriver meant that ocean-going vessels could come directly to Caerleon, moor, and offload goods from throughout the Roman world. Inevitably, the main initial concern was supply for the fortress and military outposts beyond. Eventually, however, this fundamental shift in the pattern of trade would have extended throughout the region.

Caerleon emerged as a major entrepôt for shipping. We are only beginning to understand just how important this role was.

All wrong?

Some years ago, I volunteered to help out on Dave Zienkiewicz's excavations at Celtic Manor, the hotel/golf complex where the Ryder Cup would later be held. Monsoon-like conditions were delaying progress so it was, almost literally, all hands to the pumps.

One thing raised morale, even on the wettest days. The Goldcroft Inn in Caerleon did a much-fancied meat pie; every lunch time the excavation minibus made a cross-river run for lunch! One day, in an additional attempt to raise spirits, George Boon, Keeper of Archaeology in the National Museum and previous excavator in Caerleon, came to visit. He even accompanied us for lunch and bought a round!

Boon always came over to me as an archetypal Edwardian gentleman, not in age but in demeanour. The camaraderie of the occasion didn't quite extend to joining us – he and a companion sipped half pints at the next table. He did, however, take the opportunity to sign copies of his book *Isca*. Mine is safe on the shelf behind me.

After copies had been distributed to the diggers there was a brief pause. He then rose to his feet, said 'I think we have it all wrong about Caerleon' and left. You can imagine a measure of incredulity around our table. There was a chorus of 'What? what did he say? what did he mean?' I was later on committees with George Boon. I never did find out exactly what he had in mind.

As it has transpired, however, the archaeological map of Caerleon looks a lot different today from the way it appeared in *Isca* and that is in many respects quite surprising. Caerleon has been fortunate in having a string of excavators who made major contributions to our understanding of the site specifically and Roman Wales generally over a long period of observation and excavation.

One of the earliest was John Edward Lee who, concerned with the loss of heritage that he saw around him, set about a systematic programme of investigation in the early Victorian era. His first publication went to press in 1847. I've just looked back through my own copies of his *Descriptions*, which give an account of, among other things, his exploration of the castle baths site published in 1850 and his *Isca Silurum* of 1862. He was ahead of his time. He was meticulous, provided good illustrations and was, for the time, thorough in his recording.

Lee was also instrumental in establishing a museum in Caerleon, now the National Roman Legion Museum, a part of the National Museum of Wales. He was pivotal in establishing the Caerleon Antiquarian Association, now the Monmouthshire Antiquarian Association, in 1847. As it happens, I'm the current chairman of what is the oldest local archaeological association in Wales – I'm very pleased to be associated with the tradition of John Edward Lee.

Lee had important contemporaries like Augustus Morgan, who also did valuable work in investigating and recording a range of antiquities. Others followed, including the Wheelers in the early twentieth century. Sir Mortimer Wheeler became Keeper of Archaeology in the National Museum of Wales in 1920; he was subsequently director of the museum. He excavated widely including, beginning in 1926, the important large-scale investigation of the amphitheatre in Caerleon. Much of the daily supervision on the site was undertaken by his wife, Tessa. Sir Mortimer went on to found the Institute of Archaeology within the University of London. He eventually became one of the first widely known television archaeologists.

Others followed. We've already met Victor Nash-Williams. George Boon himself did groundbreaking work in Caerleon, as did David Zienkiewicz, who excavated the fortress baths and the central tetrapylon that once dominated the fortress.

The upshot of all of this is that we have had well over 150 years of excavation, often undertaken by some of the giants of archaeology, in Caerleon. When George Boon took his leave of us in the Goldcroft, most of us would have told you that Caerleon, of all the archaeological sites in Wales, was the one that we understood best. We pretty much had this site's number.

Then, about ten years ago, Peter Guest sent some Cardiff University students to do a bit of geophysics beyond the amphitheatre in Caerleon. The surprise results led to further investigations. Based on the findings, a major excavation directed by Peter and Andrew Gardiner of the Institute of Archaeology in London began to reveal what I think can best be described as spectacular results.

Discoveries included a number of buildings including a very large apparent courtyard-style complex and, particularly important and unexpected, extensive port facilities. The known size of the fortress had suddenly grown dramatically and its critical early port facilities had been revealed. These were remarkable, previously unanticipated results, in what had been viewed as one of Britain's best-known Roman sites. We still have a lot to learn!

I think we might quibble a bit with George Boon's 'all wrong' observation. Nevertheless, there is a lot more to do even in this well-known Roman site. With that cautionary tale in mind, we'd better move on to look at some of the things that we do know. Let's start with the Roman army in the land of the Silures.

Fortress, forts and marching camps

Caerleon, Isca to the Romans, became home to the Second Augustan Legion, a permanent headquarters for nearly 200 years. As one of three permanent legionary fortresses, the other two being Chester and York, it is one of Britain's most important Roman sites.

As we have seen, Isca was built to replace the earlier fortress at Usk. Smaller forts, presumably manned by auxiliaries (non-citizen troops recruited from different parts of the empire), were established at Abergavenny (Gobannium) and Monmouth (Blestium). The presumption is that these were set up as major staging posts during the Silurian War. Other forts are known at Brecon, Pen y Gaer, Pen y Darren, Gelligaer, Caerphilly and Cardiff.

In addition, Roman armies on campaign routinely established temporary marching camps. They tended to dig in and fortify even short-term camp sites. Examples to the west of these major forts, including camps at Ystradfellte, Coelbren and Blaen Cwm Bach, have been known for some time.

What has been missing, however, are examples from what might be perceived as the heartland of the Silures. Missing, that is, until quite recently.

Toby Driver, whom we've already met, is aerial archaeologist for the Royal Commission on the Ancient and Historical Monuments of Wales. His surveys from the air have revealed a remarkable range of sites and the hot, dry summer of 2018 provided particularly good results.

Among the revelations are important previously unknown marching camps in south-east Wales. Perhaps not surprisingly, one is a small camp near Caerwent at the colourfully named Killcrow Hill near Crick. A larger site was also revealed on Llancayo Farm near Gwehelog, which may have encompassed the possible 'temple' site we have already discussed. Add to that discoveries at places like Aberllynfi near Hay and, interestingly, a possible fort near Cydweli and breath-taking seems an apt reaction.

Last year, I was pleased to be able to chair a lecture that Toby delivered to the Chepstow Archaeology Society and the Monmouthshire Antiquarian Association in a combined meeting in Chepstow. Before kick-off we were dis-cussing the exciting finds and he said to me, 'We're seeing the Silurian War!' I think he's absolutely right. Physical evidence provides graphic insight into the protracted campaigns described by Tacitus. Here's a target for further investiga-tion that can pay big dividends.

While we're at it, I'd recommend looking at another site as well. Coed y Caerau (Wood of the Forts), east of the Usk near Caerwent, is a hillfort complex that was explored with geophysical survey by one of my postgraduate students, Daryl Williams, and his wife Sam. The excellent results look very much like an 'Iron Age A', 'Iron Age B', 'Roman' sequence of occupation.

In other words, sequential Iron Age occupation may have given way to what would have been an ideal location for a Roman lookout/signalling station on an elevated site near the fortress and overlooking the Levels and the Channel beyond. This is probably a good point at which to remind you that there could well have been a Roman naval dimension to the Silurian war while monitoring shipping continued to be important in the aftermath. Exciting prospects for further inves-tigation abound!

Isca: Here to stay?

As we have seen, Tacitus tells us that the end of the Silurian War came with the campaigns of Frontinus. And we think it was he who ordered construction of Isca. Permanent occupation was probably intended from the outset, a view strengthened by the recent work done on the associated port facilities.

Isca became the military/political centre for south Wales, administering the Silurian region and beyond. A similar function was provided in the north by the fortress at Chester (Deva). It is estimated that in AD 78 there were no fewer than 30,000 Roman troops committed to Wales and its borders.

In general, Roman forts and fortresses followed a predictable pattern. In the main, Isca was a case in point. With work commencing, we think in AD 74/75, Isca was initially built with earth and timber defences, which included wooden towers built into the defensive circuit. It was then over time converted to stone.

It takes a small leap of faith but we may have a date for that conversion to stone. On prominent display in the museum in Caerleon is an impressive inscription on marble dedicated to the emperor Trajan. This skilfully well-cut inscription would have been meant for a prominent location like a gate or the central tetrapylon, presumably to mark a special occasion. It was made, according to the inscription itself, during the second consulship of Trajan. The carving is so fine and precise that David Zienkiewicz thought it might have been produced in Rome itself. If that was the case, things had changed a bit by the time the inscription arrived – Trajan had begun his third consulship.

It may be a little speculative, but it seems pretty clear to me what happened next. If you have a chance, go and have a look. You will see that a local mason had a go at updating things, adding the vertical stroke to change the II to a III. Let's just say that his efforts weren't quite up to the standard of the rest of the inscription.

Here's the leap of faith. An inscription of this size and quality must have been intended to mark an important anniversary or a special event – something like completion of the conversion of the fortress to stone, which we are pretty sure took place at about the same time. If we follow this to its logical conclusion, that wonky I actually gives us an exact calendar date of AD 100.

Returning to somewhat less speculative observations, as I've said, Isca followed the general plan for a fortress in most respects. Stone walls replaced the previous wooden defences and the towers were rebuilt in stone. The four gates were connected by two main roads, the *via praetoria* and the *via principalis*. Where Caerleon departs from the basic plan is that these roads passed through the tetrapylon as they met in the centre of the fortress.

Flanking the roads near the tetrapylon were large centrally located structures like the headquarters building, officer housing and the fortress baths. Interestingly, excavation has demonstrated that both the baths and the tetrapylon were still standing well into the Middle Ages. I've written at length about this subject, which I find fascinating. This probably isn't the time or place to pursue the topic but I'll give you some references in the notes.

Barrack blocks, one for each century of men, were located around the perimeters with large store houses, currently being investigated by Peter Guest, Andrew Gardiner and their team in the quadrant nearest the amphitheatre. Some of these features including the walls and examples of towers, barracks and the fortress baths have been consolidated and are now open to the public. So is the amphitheatre, located just outside the fortress walls. It has interesting elements like a small shrine to Nemesis opening directly onto the floor of the arena.

A civil settlement (the *canabae*) developed outside the walls as well. There also appears to have been a *colonia*, a retired veteran settlement, at Bulmore on the other side of the Usk. The road leading up toward the hillfort on Lodge Hill had cemeteries on both sides. I've had an interesting experience or two with these, which I'll share with you a little later.

You can see that not only the fortress but also a large civilian presence grew up along the banks of the Usk. The impressive, and no doubt intendedly imposing, fortress would, at full strength, have been the home base for up to 6,000 Roman soldiers. The civil settlements would probably have trebled this number.

Clearly Isca became a major population centre that was a very important element in shaping Roman south Wales. A visit to Caerleon today will help you understand just how important it was. When it comes to the interaction of Rome with the Silures, however, there is arguably an even more important site. Let's have a look at it: Caerwent, Venta Silurum, the civitas capital of the Silures, is only a relatively short distance away.

A new order: Birth of the civitas

We've seen that Venta Silurum (the market town of the Silures), modern Caerwent, became the civitas capital of the Silures. Civitas administration allowed devolution of some aspects of local administration to local communities. In practice, it was, from a Roman perspective, a good way to manage matters like collecting taxes. The system was a proven one that had worked in other parts of the empire so it is no surprise to see it being introduced in Britain. Since tribes were the polities in most of northern and western Europe, the local communities charged with operating the system were usually the extant tribes.

Other settlements, small towns, appeared as well. The army provided a ready market and not surprisingly a vicus, a civilian settlement associated with a Roman fort, often developed. There were examples at both Abergavenny and Monmouth. Such population centres were new to the region, but all were small in comparison to the capital, which at its peak, probably had some 3,000 residents. That was nothing like as many as at Isca and its 'suburbs' but it was large in its local context.

Not surprisingly, much of Caerwent was given over to housing, with large courtyard town houses dominating much of the periphery of its enclosed area. Temples were also built both in the town and just outside it. The commercial life of Caerwent (Venta) revolved around what's best described as a 'High Street' running east–west right through the centre of the town.

Strip houses, with living accommodation behind shops facing onto the high street, dominated this central area, along with the forum that is best thought of as a market square, probably replete with both permanent shops and temporary stalls selling a wide range of produce. Rising over the forum on its north side was the basilica, a sort of 'town hall', the largest building in the town. The basilica would have been an administrative and judicial centre not only for the town but also for the surrounding area. The curia, the tribal senate of the Silures, met in the basilica.

There is little doubt that Venta Silurum provides us with a sort of litmus test for relations between the indigenous population and the invading/occupying Roman army. Since that relationship is central to our main themes, it's something that we need to look at carefully. We can't be certain of the exact nature of the early post-conquest interaction between the Silures and Rome. To an extent, no doubt, the indigenous population would have been both dismayed and perplexed at the new order being imposed.

I'm not sure, however, how far we should take the 'fractured society' model. For example, I'm struck by the amount of apparently non-Roman horse gear that has been found in early Romano-British contexts. A particularly interesting piece is held by the National Museum. A copper alloy strap union, it was found at the Maendy Camp site. It may be late in date and it may point to a sort of cultural fusion.

The red and yellow enamel design on the strap union is colourful and is reminiscent, in some respects, of items that we have already discussed. However, the pattern is more balanced and as a consequence arguably more classical in form; this is not a La Tène design. When looking at items like this, I can't help noting an apparent mixing of styles while at the same time wondering if the equestrian elite of the Silures might have been a bit more resilient than you would have expected.

Whatever the best interpretation of this sort of material might be, the creation of the civitas remains pivotal to our understanding of relations in the region. For a long time, lacking sufficient evidence to know, there were two popular views about how the process might have taken place.

These contrasting ideas presented another of those really good games you could play with undergraduates. Classes could be asked which interpretation they preferred and why. One school of thought was that Frontinus was quite 'enlightened' and he could see that some sort of new relationship with the native population was needed. Consequently, he moved to establish a civitas straight away. Let's call this the 'early civitas' model.

Those who were sceptical responded that after the struggle of a quarter-century-long guerrilla war, time was needed before the Romans would risk trusting these people with any form of local government. The civitas could only have come after a lengthy transitional period during which the army exercised direct supervision and control. This gives us a 'late civitas' model. I found that classes usually divided about 50/50 on the matter; there were champions of both models.

At that time, there was general agreement that there was a good way to answer the question. The thinking was basically this. If the civitas required an ordo, a tribal senate/regional council, and the ordo sat in a basilica, dating the construction of the basilica could go a long way toward dating the civitas itself.

This is where matters stood when Richard Brewer, who became Keeper of Archaeology in the National Museum, began extensive research excavations in the town. An early target was one of those courtyard houses, in this case, replete with such luxurious features as a hypocaust, an underfloor central heating system.

When this excavation was successfully completed, Richard turned his attention to an even bigger project – the forum basilica itself. Rather like Caerleon, Caerwent had been the focus of investigations for over a century. Excavations between 1899 and 1913 had largely revealed a ground plan of the town including the location of the forum and basilica. Subsequent work by Wheeler, Nash-Williams and W.F. Grimes had added to the picture. Much of the earliest excavation, however, had simply established the outlines of buildings in the latest phases of the town and did not, in most cases, provide much helpful information about use, building sequences, construction dates, etc. In 1984, Richard began addressing the problem.

My role in this excavation was purely that of spectator – but I was a keen spectator. Knowing many members of the team and being very interested, I was a regular visitor to the site. And I had my timing worked out perfectly.

Early on I noticed that the doughnut van arrived daily just at morning break time. Archaeologists clearly made good customers! Consequently, I timed my visits to coincide with the arrival of the van, sometimes following it onto site. As a way to have a quick update on progress, I can recommend a chat over coffee and doughnuts.

The excavation provided excellent results, including the revelation of the curia chamber itself with evidence of its mosaic central pavement flanked by cross benches. The chamber has been consolidated and is open to the public. I recommend a visit; when you're there look out for the platform bases where the two magistrates would have presided. You will also see the slots for the bases of the cross benches. Should you imagine 'parliamentary noises' being exchanged, I wonder?

Excavation of the forum basilica at Caerwent. This is one of several of those 'game-changing' excavations discussed in the text. (National Museum of Wales)

The now fully excavated and open to the public 'senate chamber' of the civitas Silurum. (National Museum of Wales)

All of this was interesting and exciting. To find the construction date, however, you had to find dateable material securely sealed on the construction horizon. You don't need me to explain that the construction horizon is at the bottom. If you are carefully excavating and recording the layers above, working your way through different lenses of occupation and use, you are not going to find the date you want quickly.

In fact, if the careful, large-scale summer excavation takes a decade plus to complete, which it did, you have to be very patient indeed. Eventually, however, the construction levels were revealed and both definition of features and dateable material were excellent.

So, now we know. Construction of the basilica took place during the late Trajanic or early Hadrianic period – in other words, it was built in about AD 120. The basilica and, presumably the establishment of the civitas, come some fifty years after the end of the war. I think that makes sense. There are minor differences in the way experts like to 'date' generations. By most people's reckoning that's two-and-a-bit generations. Probably enough time for the Silures to have adjusted to the new regime and for the Romans to be ready to relax their grip.

Town and country

Caerwent must have become quite a cosmopolitan town, at least for its place and time. High-ranking members of the tribal leadership would have been present in some numbers. At the same time, the inscriptions that we have already discussed suggest a retired veteran presence as well as people from, or at least influenced by, other parts of the empire.

This cultural blending is reflected in artefact assemblages with, for example, ceramics from a variety of production centres. There are local pottery products; not that long ago interesting and slightly surprising evidence of one local production centre came in the form of a large kiln, still containing its final firing, which was excavated before disappearing under one of the greens on the Celtic Manor golf course.

There is also a quantity of diagnostic black burnished pottery, a British product made to sell to, among others, the soldiers of the legion. At the other end of the luxury scale, there are also many examples of material like samian ware. This was very fine hard-fired red gloss pottery. Sometimes called *terra sigillata*, samian ware, made mainly in Gaul, was an important luxury trade item. It was often decorated with intricate stamped designs of everything from animal and vegetal images through to gods, goddesses, gladiators, etc. Because of the distinctive decorative styles, it is frequently fairly closely dateable. Often makers put their stamp on the base of vessels. If you have the maker's name, it can be very dateable indeed.

Other assemblages tell similar stories. Brooches from Caerwent, for example, came in a range of styles with both hints of native influence as well as classical design. There is a good display of some of these in Newport Museum. It's worth a visit.

Examples of cultural interaction contribute to the image of Caerwent as a pretty diverse place and there was no lack of romanitas (Roman-ness) in the town. Examples of Roman lifestyles could also be found in the countryside where a villa economy emerged, at least in some places.

An area where several villas have been known for some time is the fertile Vale of Glamorgan. Examples include sites at or near Ely, Llandoc, Llantwit Major and Whitton. Whitton is often presented as a clear demonstration of the 'march of romanitas'.

Excavated between 1965 and 1970 by Mike Jarrett and Stuart Wrathmell, Whitton appears to have begun as a pre-conquest farm with roundhouses in a banked enclosure. This late Iron Age plan looks to have continued for eighty years or so. Then in the early second century AD, two new buildings were erected, apparently employing the same basic construction techniques. These later buildings were, however, square in plan.

Then, by the middle of the second century, stone footings and a hypocaust were constructed. Building and rebuilding on the site continued into the fourth century. The later buildings were wholly Roman in inspiration. These results seemed to point to a pattern of gradual embracing of Roman lifestyles. The natives were no longer 'restless'; instead they were gradually becoming Romans.

Evidence of a villa system has been emerging closer to Caerwent as well. Once again, Toby Driver and his aerial surveys has been a key factor in expanding our list of sites. A villa on the military facility immediately to the north of Caerwent, initially the Royal Navy Propellant Factory, has been known for years. Now other confirmed or suspected examples have been found at Five Lanes, Llanwern, Rogiet, Dewstow Farm and Great Pencarn Farm, all on the Levels relatively near to Caerwent.

In 1998 there was excavation at Great Pencarn farm as part of the Glamorgan-Gwent Archaeological Trust's Romano-British south-east Wales lowland settlement survey.

As we have seen, the clearly defined apparent villa on the Wyndcliff and associated features, probably Iron Age in date, must be high on our list for future investigation.

At this stage, you may be picturing a steady advance of romanitas, at least in the most desirable agricultural areas like the Levels and the Vale. Don't make your mind up too soon.

Other sites in the Vale, notably Biglis near Barry, tell a slightly different story. Here three Romano-British phases of occupation were identified, lasting well into the fourth century and possibly longer. As far as could be ascertained, accommodation was provided by sub-circular timber-frame buildings throughout. There were, however, Roman coins and ceramics as well as a quite sophisticated Roman-style corn-drying kiln. Here, people seem to have been picking and choosing, embracing Roman goods and practices when and if it suited them but still preferring a roundhouse as home.

Two of the sites near Caerwent that have been identified by aerial survey, Langstone and Trewen, seem best described simply as farmsteads, at least at present. That certainly is the case with the excavated Caerwent Quarry site less than a mile south-east of the civitas capital. Here occupation began in the second half of the first century AD and it began with roundhouses. It remained in use into the fourth century and possibly beyond with, as far as we can tell, the occupants still in roundhouses.

This sequence fits in well with that of one of the most fully understood rural farmsteads, Thornwell Farm near Chepstow. This site isn't in the shadow of Caerwent in the same way that the quarry is, but it's pretty close. Excavations here directed by Gwilym Hughes and published in 1992, present a fascinating sequence of occupation.

Six main occupation phases were identified in an excavation at the farm site, which is near the Welsh end of the old Severn Bridge; it had been designated as the location for a new large housing estate, prompting the excavation.

Activity at Thornwell Farm began in the late Bronze Age and was characterised by a large roundhouse. A new roundhouse was built in the early Iron Age and by the next phase drystone walls partially enclosed two closely spaced roundhouses. These seem to date from the very late Iron Age or even from the conquest period.

An additional roundhouse appeared later associated with occupation from the late first/early second century. A final confirmed phase dates from the third century, extending into the mid-fourth century, possibly even later. During this period, there were up to four circular buildings, two of which couldn't be contemporary because the footings of one cut through those of the other.

The point to stress here is that, as the excavator notes in the final report, 'the character and appearance of the settlement did not noticeably change throughout the Roman period'. If not literally in its shadow, at least very close to the civitas capital, the people at this site were pursuing a native lifestyle while living in roundhouses right through the entire Roman era.

Fewer upland sites have been investigated but the picture emerging is that away from the capital, lifestyle may not have changed very much at all. Indeed, settlement patterns in south Wales may have generally followed a different pattern from that of more Romanised regions to the east. Unlike some places like the Somerset and Avon Levels, there seems to have been little tendency toward nucleation in south Wales; sites were more dispersed, often favouring defensive positions.

This was put succinctly by Pete Insoll who, having conducted a comparative study, suggested that in the west the end of Roman Britain may not have had the impact that might have been expected. He wrote 'contrasting settlement patterns persist, suggesting cultural continuity and hinting that the social and economic landscape may have been less fundamentally affected by the Roman withdrawal'.

It seems likely that in some rural areas, romanitas may have been something of a veneer. Away from the influence of population centres like Caerwent and Caerleon with its canabae and colonia, it may have been a very thin veneer indeed.

Even in the civitas capital, however, emerging Roman lifestyles do not appear to have been all-inclusive. The buildings and layout of the town were certainly Roman in inspiration. That is also true of the ordo, the tribal senate. However, don't forget the Paulinus inscription and the nature of that senate. Action was being taken on the authority of a *tribal* council of the civitas of the Silures. Tribal identity and consequently a measure of tribal structure survived.

As we have also seen, there is conclusive evidence of conflation with religious imagery literally fusing Roman and native tradition. And keep in mind things like the little mother goddess and the antefixa from Caerleon with imagery that, as Miranda reminds us, 'appears to owe more to Silurian than Roman tradition'. Above all, perhaps, remember that stone head from Caerwent. Raised on its altar-like platform, this purely native cult object was being revered in the civitas capital in the fourth century.

With communities living in roundhouses in view of Venta, and purely Iron Age in spirit devotional objects being honoured in the capital itself at the very end of Roman Britain, it seems fair to say that native traditions remained strong in Siluria. I don't want to overstate the case. There was clearly romanitas and cultural change. Nevertheless, the balance between Roman and native tradition may have been less clear cut than has often been suggested.

There are, however, important aspects of Roman tradition that outlasted the last of the legions. Let's move on and look at a couple of important ones.

A new order?

There are at least two areas in which we can point to significant and lasting change. Even with one of these, however, there are important mixed messages that we should try to understand.

In terms of culture and society, it is hard to overstate the importance of language and religion. Rome and Roman influences had an important impact on both in Siluria. Let's look at language first.

Here's a simplified version of a complex process that I think helped undergraduates grasp the fundamentals of a process. A question that is often asked is, 'What language did Iron Age peoples in Britain speak? Were the Silures, the Brigantes, the Iceni and Catuvellauni able to understand one another?'

There is a lot here that is not fully understood, but for the sake of argument let's start with the pretty safe assumption that all these people spoke a Brythonic version of a Celtic language. Given modern variations in dialect and accent, however, it's hard not to think that they might have found one another a bit challenging to understand at times.

For ease of understanding, it is sometimes helpful to think of these related languages as 'Old British'. With the Roman conquest and subsequent administration, there were soon significant influences on native speech from Latin, the language of Roman administration. An element of Latinisation brought changes and we are left with what we may choose to describe as 'New British'. This is important because, by the end of the Romano-British period New British was evolving – evolving into Old Welsh.

Not surprisingly, there is quite a lot of Latin in modern Welsh. Obvious examples include building/construction terms like *ffenestr* (window) and *mur* (wall). Some examples are a little more difficult to explain like *ffos* (ditch) – there was obviously a perfectly acceptable native word for ditch. Perhaps looking at the formidable ditches around sites like the fortress at Isca was a factor.

The same is probably true of a particularly obvious example. *Pont* (bridge) is a term encountered regularly in modern Welsh. Just think of place names like Pontypridd, Pontypool, Pen y Bont, etc. You will probably have noticed in the last of those examples, the Welsh for Bridgend, *pont* has mutated, just reminding you that we are still dealing with a Celtic language. The Romans were good engineers and they made impressive bridges. I expect there was a tendency to say 'OK, if they call that a pont, pont it is'.

To sum up, Latin influenced language in the Silurian region as it did in many, arguably most, of Europe. What it didn't do, however, was transform the language completely. The process did not lead to a new Romance language. Romance languages are those that are so fully Latinised that they form a closely related family of languages. Major examples include Italian, Spanish, Portuguese, French, Romanian and Catalan.

If we are trying to assess the degree of romanitas, the legacy of Romanisation in Siluria, we need to stress this point. At the end of the Roman period, we still have a people speaking a recognisably Celtic language, not a Romance one. That must be telling us something pretty important about the question.

Lasting change?

At this point, you might be asking yourself if there was any lasting legacy at all. There was! And the nature of arguably the most durable element in that legacy might surprise you.

We need to think about religion because that was an area where the legacy of Rome remains strong to this day. You may be thinking that this seems unlikely – people in early medieval Wales didn't spend a lot of time worshipping Jupiter or Mars. Remind yourself, however, that as the Roman imperial presence declined in Britain, neither did many Romans. A new religion was growing to the point that it would become the official religion of the Roman Empire in the late fourth century. Rome was embracing Christianity.

This was a slow process; we have already discussed Roman antipathy to the early Christians. We know the names of three early martyrs in Britain. One was Alban; the other two, Julius and Aaron, died in Caerleon. Gildas, a useful if uneven source for early medieval British history, wrote in the early sixth century that a martyrium near Caerleon commemorated them.

By the fourth century, however, the influence of Christianity was growing rapidly. This is neither the time nor place to pursue the topic in depth but the upturn in fortune owed a great deal to Constantine. Son of one of the four emperors in the 'tetrarchy', proclaimed emperor in York, he secured this position with victory at the Milvian Bridge on the outskirts of Rome in AD 312.

We are told that he credited his victory to the intervention of the Christian God, whose symbol he had his troops paint on their shields after he had a vision. In the aftermath, he moved quickly to establish what was called the 'Peace of the Church' in AD 313. This ended persecution and granted Christians legal protection throughout the empire.

Influence and power were increasingly transferred to Christian bishops and, even though the emperor delayed his own formal conversion for some time, Christianity continued to grow in influence, becoming the official religion by AD 380.

It is likely that Christianity already had many converts in Britain by the time of Constantine. It is interesting to see that when a major church council was held in Arles in AD 314, it was attended by three British bishops and representatives of a fourth. In other words, hard on the heels of the Peace of the Church, an episcopal structure was already in place in Britain.

A centre of this emergence of Christianity may well have been the civitas of the Silures. I'm taken by George Boon's interpretation of the excavation of a courtyard town house in Caerwent. Conversion in the fourth century had seen a group of rooms modified to, among other things, add an apse to the larger central space.

There was a plain red mosaic floor and the general arrangement of the new plan led Boon to suggest, on the basis of comparison with other known early Christian sites, that these could have included a baptistery. In other words, this townhouse had been converted to a 'house church' in keeping with contemporary Christian practice.

This potential emergence as a Christian centre would be interesting in its own right. It is particularly so if Boon was right with the baptistery explanation. In this early period, baptism required a bishop.

The chi rho imagery reputedly revealed by George Boon's thumb. However it was rediscovered, it reminds us that by the end of Roman Britain, Christianity was the religion of Rome. (National Museum of Wales)

Arguably even more compelling evidence of another house church came from an excavation in 1906. Heated by a hypocaust, this courtyard house revealed a large urn buried into the floor of one of the rooms opening onto the ambulatory that gave access to the courtyard. The urn was capped by an overturned mortarium, a distinctive sort of Roman mixing bowl. The urn contained a pewter bowl and plate with other objects including three red ceramic bowls and fragments of woollen twill cloth.

The excavator at the time suggested that this material had the look of a Christian cache. Indeed, the utensils seemed right for celebration of *agape*, a supper of 'friendly affection' observed by early Christians. It seemed a reasonable interpretation but it needed a bit of confirmatory evidence to feel confident about it. That is, until 1961 when the material was re-examined.

As we have been considering a range of subjects in this book, I've allowed myself to digress with the odd story. So far, they have all been personal accounts of things I've been directly involved in or at least observed. Consequently, I have to insert a disclaimer at this point. What I'm about to tell you may be apocryphal. It was, however, told to me as a true story by people who should know.

The re-examination of the material in 1961 was a bit early for me. I'm told, however, that George Boon was in the basement of the museum having a look at the artefact assemblage. He is said to have stared critically at the pewter bowl. Then, licking a thumb, said 'This hasn't been cleaned very well.'

As he rubbed a smudge away, what was revealed was the chi rho symbol. Incised on the bottom of the bowl was the distinctive monogram made of the first two letters of the Greek work *Christos*. Here was the evocative symbol of early Christianity inscribed on a bowl in the civitas capital in the fourth century!

Groundbreaking discoveries come in all sorts of different ways.

10

Not very dark at all

Through the years I've written quite a bit about south-east Wales in the fifth to seventh centuries. It's a period that I find fascinating so I'm going to have to try to be a bit restrained and concentrate on some key issues. What we are most interested in at this point in our discussions is what the evidence can tell us about cultural change and/or cultural continuity.

To begin with, let's start with what we should call this period. Perhaps more to the point is what we shouldn't call it. As I've tried to persuade many students over a number of years, the old favourite 'Dark Ages' is best avoided.

The description conjures up an image of decline and ultimately collapse with the ending of Roman Britain, often presented is a picture of a grim illiteracy accompanying cultural decline. Don't be too quick to embrace this image. The surviving evidence may be a bit patchy but through monastic tracts and other records we know that this is not a good description of society in the west.

A far better description, which is accurate while not being prejudicial, is simply Early Medieval. To my mind, early here describes the period between the end of Roman control and the Norman conquest. Early Medieval Wales, particularly in the south-east, was literate and for the time we're looking at quite stable. So, let's leave it at Early Medieval and move on.

Back to the future (or at least the hillfort)?

One of the most interesting revelations from our excavation of the Lodge Hill hillfort was that it had been reoccupied. As we saw in Chapter 7, the entrance that had been filled in was at some point reinstated. This reopening of the entrance couldn't be dated but it appears to have happened late in the occupation sequence of the site. What can be dated, at least roughly, are the sherds of Roman pottery as well as brick and tile fragments recovered in the excavation.

The pottery assemblage was examined by Peter Webster, who identified three sherds of samian ware among the finds. Particularly interesting, however, was the rim of a black burnished bowl that was a form of pot belonging to a period dating from 'about AD 270 or later'. Sherds from a mortarium also came from a third- or fourth-century vessel probably made in or near Cirencester. In general, as we said in the report, the Romano-British material reflects a bias toward the third/fourth centuries.

This tentative date range is interesting, particularly if we consider the situation in the area in the late third century. We have seen how Caerleon had served as the headquarters of the Second Augustan Legion for some two centuries. By the late third century, however, Roman priorities, and as a consequence their military organisation, were changing. Coastal defence was becoming increasingly important. Indeed, when the military commander Carausius, ostensibly resisting coastal raiders, established a rebel regime in AD 286 the whole of Britain effectively became an independent entity and remained so until AD 296.

With instability growing in Britain, shore forts became the new base for troops during the late Roman period. In south Wales, the fort at Cardiff increasingly assumed that role. As the shore forts developed, the old legionary fortresses declined and ultimately were abandoned.

It seems clear that this was the fate of Isca, where fourth-century occupation appears to have been only by civilians. We don't know the exact date when the last troops left Caerleon but it is generally believed to have been in the late third century. Indeed, 'about AD 270 or later' might be a pretty good guess. In other words, it looks a strong possibility that when or shortly after the army left Caerleon, someone began to occupy the hillfort above the abandoned fortress straight away.

At this point, let's do a bit of speculating. There are all sorts of reasons why this might have happened and we don't know which explanation is best. However, there has been a suggestion that I find quite attractive.

Cast your mind back to the arrival of the Romans and the associated land confiscation to create a territorium for the legion. Large tracts of fertile agricultural land in the Usk Valley were lost to the native population. Now with the army gone, this highly desirable farm land was presumably up for grabs.

It's an attractive idea that a lingering memory might still link the hillfort with the land. The imposing symbol of pre-conquest society could retain potency for the people of the area. I like the idea that reoccupying the hillfort might be seen to be a way to stake a claim on the land below it.

If that was the case, it could help explain a plethora of reoccupied hillforts throughout Wales with good examples from the Silurian region during the late Roman and Early Medieval periods. As we saw in the last chapter, in the west of

Britain there seems to have been a growing preference for defended sites. In a number of cases, these defended sites were the hillforts themselves.

Interestingly, archaeological investigation has indicated that there were some hillforts that weren't abandoned in the first place. A case in point is Caer Dynnaf near Cowbridge in the Vale of Glamorgan. Here a half dozen or so farms were located in the hillfort enclosure and occupied through most, if not all, of the Romano-British period.

If that surprises you, have a go at explaining the Llwynheirnin site near Llansamlet. Here, not only was Roman pottery found, it was found sealed, incorporated into the fabric of the rampart. The easiest way to account for this material is to conclude that the hillfort was built, or at least rebuilt, after the conquest.

Roman ceramics have been found on a number of sites in Glamorgan and, as we have seen, at Llanmelin and Sudbrook near the civitas capital at Caerwent itself. Lodge Hill fits well into this model of hillfort occupation/reoccupation.

Given that enclosed defensive sites were becoming important again, we need to have a closer look at an excavated site that is, in many respects, Iron Age in appearance and inspiration, but which was purpose-built in the early medieval period. This means turning our attention to Dinas Powys, an enclosed high-status site located on a limestone ridge in the eastern Vale of Glamorgan near Cardiff.

Excavations at Dinas Powys were directed by Leslie Alcock from 1954 to 1958. Within an enclosure formed by revetted banks and ditches, drip gullies defined two sub-rectangular early medieval buildings. These buildings are generally interpreted as a hall and a barn.

What makes the site of particular interest is the range of artefact assemblages, particularly ceramics, which suggests occupation between the fifth and seventh centuries. Dinas Powys, with new investigations led by Andy Seaman and Alan Lane in 2011–14, has, along with Tintagel, emerged as one of Britain's key Early Medieval high-status type sites.

As I've just suggested, the thing that makes Dinas Powys especially significant is the large and varied amount of pottery recovered. I've had the opportunity to examine this material in detail. I should explain that a sort of 'mythic' mist, with hints of Arthurian associations, surrounded Lodge Hill before we began excavations there, raising at least the possibility of reoccupation.

Because of this, Josh Pollard and I decided it would be a good idea to get our eye in before starting, so we decamped to the reserve collection in Cardiff and went through the lot. I'll be honest with you, when you are about halfway through the bags of coarse ware sherds, you tend to think that there are more exciting ways to spend an afternoon in Cardiff.

There is, however, no doubting the exciting message that these sherds convey. For example, there were over eighty fragments of fine red slip wares, some with stamped or rouletted decoration. Many are what are called Phocaean slip wares and at a distance they look a bit like samian, the *terra sigillata*, which we have already discussed. On closer examination, however, the more porous fabric tells us that we are dealing with something quite different.

We are also dealing with something sufficiently distinctive to show where they came from and it is this that tends to produce a sharp intake of breath. Some of these red slip wares were produced in Asia Minor and there are examples from both the eastern Mediterranean and from around Carthage in modern Tunisia. There are similar indications from the over 170 sherds of amphorae, many of which originated in the eastern Mediterranean. At least one fabric is that of an amphora produced in what is today Syria.

Among those bags of grey wares in the National Museum are examples from western France, with some having been produced in the Bordeaux region. There was also quite a lot of glass, representing at least forty different vessels. These seem to have been Anglo-Saxon imports.

I'm sure you can see straight away just how important this material is. I wouldn't for a moment try to persuade you that those in charge at Dinas Powys were trading directly with the eastern Mediterranean and beyond. However, that isn't really the point. They were clearly involved, over a considerable period of time, with a trade network that extended as far as places like Syria.

That improves our perspective on the Early Medieval west. Not such a dark age after all!

The 'running felines', a decorated pot fragment from the key Early Medieval site at Dinas Powys. Many of my students have been reluctant to accept the feline description, preferring rabbits or a wide range of alternative small mammals. Look closely and decide for yourself! (National Museum of Wales)

Llys and llan

When Alcock wrote up his findings over fifty years ago, he suggested that a good description of Dinas Powys was as a 'proto-llys'. I quite like that description and see no reason not to continue to describe it as exactly that.

Llys in modern Welsh is a court; it is best to think of a princely court in the early medieval context. It can be seen as an administrative centre in a system that may seem a little complicated if you aren't used to it.

Basically, Early Medieval land tenure in Wales revolved around a fiscal unit called a maenor. In what is probably an idealised model, each maenor was subdivided into four trefi. Now, just to confuse you, in modern Welsh *tref* (*trefi* if you have more than one of them) is a town. For the period we're looking at, think of it as a farm of approximately 120 acres. Interestingly the term villa is also used in early documentation, apparently synonymous with tref.

There were other units, both larger and smaller, such as cantref, literally a hundred trefi. Similarly, you had pentrefi (still do – it means village today). You have already encountered hafod and hendref when we looked at transhumance. These seem to have been important elements in the Early Medieval landscape as well.

For now, let's try to keep things fairly simple and concentrate on the llys. Except to make sense of the court we need to consider another element, the llan. In many cases, it increasingly appears to be in most cases, the secular llys was accompanied by a religious centre, the llan. The term originally described the sub-circular enclosure around the church; it is now synonymous with the church itself.

Dinas Powys is a good case in point. About a mile from the site that we are calling a proto-llys is the church of St Dochdwy in Llandoc. An early cross base in the churchyard points to an early foundation. This is confirmed by the associated, now excavated, cemetery.

To the south of the church is the site of a Roman villa. In the 1990s, when planning consent was given for a housing estate between the two, excavation revealed no fewer than 858 burials in a curvilinear enclosure. The inhumations date from throughout the Early Medieval period with radiocarbon date ranges from the AD 500s to nearly AD 1000.

Not surprisingly in what was presumably a Christian cemetery, there were few grave goods. Particularly telling, however, were sherds of amphorae, olive oil containers from Asia Minor. These trade goods have direct parallels with the assemblage from Dinas Powys and suggest close association between the secular site and its ecclesiastical neighbour. It appears to be an excellent example of llys and llan that seems to have been replicated at many locations across south Wales.

Within this system there were larger religious centres and Llandoc is probably an example of one of the clas churches that were made up of a 'community' of frequently hereditary canons or resident priests. If the hereditary bit gives you pause for thought, it's worth remembering that the church that emerged in Wales was Christian but it wasn't Roman Catholic. There were a number of significant differences.

Among the important and highly influential early monastic centres were Llanilltud Fawr (Llantwit Major) and Llancarfan. Another example, which we need to consider in some depth, is Caerwent, the capital of the civitas. It's a site that seems to have taken on a rather different role in the Early Medieval period.

From civitas to kingdom

It is generally thought that Venta Silurum, Caerwent, began as an undefended 'ribbon development'. In the late second century, however, defences were erected at Caerwent along with many other larger towns in Britain. These took the form of earthwork banks topped by a timber palisade.

In about AD 330, presumably reflecting growing instability possibly in part arising from the coastal threat that we discussed previously, stone walls were built in front of the existing banks. These walls are thought to have been some 25ft (7.6m) in height and in many places still stand to 17ft (5.2m). Not long after construction of the walls, probably around AD 350, stone towers were added to the north and south walls. Interestingly, these towers are very similar to those at the increasingly important fort at Cardiff.

Stone-built gates controlled access to the town, with the main east and west gates providing a double arched 'carriageway' flanked by square towers. There were smaller, single-arched, gates on the north and south. It is, no doubt, instructive that at some point in the late Roman period, the north gate was blocked although a small doorway was retained, presumably for pedestrian access. The south gate, on the other hand, was blocked completely.

There is plenty of evidence for late Roman and Early Medieval occupation in Caerwent. Artefacts like penannular brooches and other items of personal adornment, for example, are pretty diagnostic. The best evidence, however, comes from two large, partially excavated cemeteries.

One of these was actually in the town, extending around today's parish church. It seems to have been in use for some time as some of the graves respect the 'footprint' of Roman buildings while others cut across demolished walls. One was actually cut into the 'High Street', the main east–west road. The radiocarbon date for the burial in the road was between AD 540 and 770.

A second cemetery was located just outside the east gate. Inhumations had been found here in 1910 so construction of retirement homes for clergy led to further excavation in 1973. Over 100 additional burials were revealed with radiocarbon dates from the fourth to the ninth century. It is apparent that Caerwent continued to be

'Good and lofty'? A bastion built into the south wall at Caerwent. (Ray Howell)

occupied, and presumably continued to be important, through much of the Early Medieval period. Interestingly, though, this settlement may have been largely monastic.

The *Vitae Sanctorum Britanniae* (*Lives of British Saints*) credits establishment of a monastery in the town to a monk named Tatheus or Tathan. It seems that the king of the emerging realm of Gwent had decamped to his llys at nearby Portskewett, probably originally Porth Is Coed for reasons we'll consider shortly, close to Sudbrook Camp.

The king granted land comprising 'the good, fertile, lofty, noble city of Caerwent'. That description may well sound a bit much for commuters who know it today only by driving past on the modern A48. But drive round to the south wall and stand under the best preserved of those towers and I think you might say that 'good, fertile and lofty' actually sounds about right.

Kings and kingdoms

The void created by the end of Roman Britain, officially AD 410 but in practice no doubt a long and protracted process rather than a single event, was filled by regional kingdoms. These grew up throughout Wales; in what had once been the land of the Silures, the two largest were Gwent and Glamorgan. The latter, western, kingdom, originally Glywysing, took the name of a king named Morgan, i.e. Morgannwg (modern Welsh) – Glamorgan (in English derived from Gwlad Morgan). We need to give some thought to the eastern kingdom, Gwent.

There are later medieval accounts of the early Welsh kingdoms and a handful of contemporary accounts. In one of these we find Gildas describing a king named Vortipor, whose grave stone survives, as the 'tyrant of the Demetae'.

It's very interesting to see the tribal name surviving in this account and we have to wonder if there are similar instances in Siluria. The initial response might be no. But let's not be hasty – as I've said, we need to revisit the kingdom of Gwent.

We have seen that the tribal capital of the Silures during the Roman period was Venta Silurum, the market town of the Silures. We have also seen that over time the town became Caerwent, as it is today.

To help understand how that came about, remember that the emerging vernacular was evolving from 'New British' to 'Old Welsh'. Also remind yourself that in Welsh caer is fort. As far as we know, Caerwent was always a market town and never a fort. We might want to be slightly cautious with that conclusion as fourth-century finds like distinctive decorated belt buckles and *plumbata,* barbed projectiles, may suggest some sort of late garrison.

Whether or not that was the case, the high stone walls and projecting towers make Caerwent look like it ought to have been a fort whether it was or not. Certainly, it began to be referred to as one – Venta Silurum, Caer Venta Silurum, Caer Venta, Caerwent. We have a tendency to shorten thing in speech and to run things together. It's a natural sequence leading to Caerwent.

But what if we want to start talking about it as the fort? You've already seen the process of mutation in a previous chapter so you may not be surprised that putting in 'the' ('y'), can produce a mutation from Caerwent to Y Gaerwent. Now, do that running things together bit and see where it gets you. It's an easy shortcut to Gwent, the kingdom emerging in the land of the Silures!

There's a related point that I think is really important. You remember that king of Gwent who established his llys at Portskewett. I suggested that the name of the llys might derive from Porth Is Coed (there are other suggestions but let's think about this one). Early Welsh kingdoms were fairly fluid concepts with subdivisions, and subkingdoms were common. The main subdivisions in Gwent were Gwynllŵg in the west, Gwent Uwchcoed (Gwent above the wood, i.e. Wentwood) and Gwent Iscoed (Gwent below the wood, i.e. the area surrounding Caerwent that included Portskewett).

That king granting land to Tathan is the earliest king of Gwent whose name we know. His name was Caradoc ap Ynyr, sometimes called Caradoc Freichfas. Caradoc/Caradog is the Welsh version of Caratacus.

So, as the kingdom of Venta Silurum was emerging, the name of the great resistance leader at the start of the Silurian War was not only remembered; it was remembered as a name fit for a king. I think that is telling us a great deal.

11

Face to face?

As we move closer to the end of this book, we need to begin to draw some conclusions. I hope that one thing we can agree on straight away is that the Silures were a fascinating early people. In the next chapter, I want us to look at ways we might be able to understand them better.

For now, however, I'd like to think a bit about legacy before we move on to a couple of new and exciting discoveries. With respect to legacy, in the last chapter, I hinted at a measure of political continuity in the emergence of the Early Medieval kingdoms. There is also a sense of folk memory that may be reflected in medieval literature. John Koch, in particular, has argued that elements in sources like the tales of the Mabinogi, more commonly referred to as the *Mabinogion*, have demonstrable roots in the Iron Age. Another possible example may be the sixth-century Welsh poem *Gododdin*, attributed to the poet Aneirin and written somewhere in what is now the Scottish borders.

If that last bit sounds surprising, remember that Welsh was once spoken much more widely than it is today. It's also worth stressing that of all the legacies that we can demonstrate, the Welsh language is arguably the most important. The Silures may not have spoken Welsh as we know it but they spoke an antecedent that led to the language spoken today.

It's worth noting that references to these earlier times and this particular early people keep cropping up through history. I know this is cherry-picking but while writing this chapter, I leafed through an early source that was readily to hand – Percy Enderbie's *Cambria Triumphans* of 1661 – just to check. It didn't take long to establish that he knew his Tacitus well enough to describe the Silures with 'their natural boldnesse' under the leadership of 'Caraticus'. He also described the campaign of Frontinus against the Silures, fighting not only the warlike tribesmen but also the mountains and other 'places of very great and difficult accesse [*sic*]'.

And such accounts continued to resonate in the land of the Silures. This is not the time or place for any sort of meaningful discussion of the complexities of medieval and Early Modern Welsh literature. As with previous chapters, however, in the notes I've pointed you toward some sources that might help if you want to pursue the topic further.

For our purposes here, let's just say that generally, and particularly in south Wales, the Silures tend to linger in the collective imagination. They seem to lurk somewhere in the back of many people's minds. It strikes me as pretty instructive, for example, that when, in the early nineteenth century, unrest in the industrial valleys of Gwent and Glamorgan led to widespread social disorder, disorder sometimes described by modern historians as an attempted revolution, a stated objective was the creation of a 'Silurian Republic'.

Recent discoveries

Shortly after publication of *Searching for the Silures*, in which I alluded to that Silurian Republic, new research excavations began in Caerleon. We have already discussed the quite remarkable discoveries arising from the exploration of the extramural port facilities and related infrastructure near the amphitheatre.

In a sense, these discoveries represented a spin-off from research excavations that started in 2007 in the Priory Field within the fortress. For some time, we have had a fairly complete plan of the fortress but parts of that plan, particularly in the quadrant nearest the amphitheatre, were a bit speculative.

Based on limited investigation and analogy with other fortresses, this was shown as the location for granaries and other store buildings. Peter Guest, then of Cardiff University, and Andrew Gardner of UCL started work to test the accuracy of the plan while improving our understanding of a comparatively under-investigated area of the fortress.

Geophysical survey was followed by targeted excavation. Whereas the work on the port complex caused a major rethink about the development of the fortress, the Priory Field produced more predictable results; evidence of structures included a large store building that became a focus of excavation.

The site may have behaved predictably with respect to the plan but that doesn't make it any less interesting or important. Indeed, some of the finds, like remarkably intact Roman armour, quite rightly caused considerable excitement.

What excited me most, however, was something totally unexpected. Mark Lewis of the National Museum was providing specialist expertise with finds on the excavation and it was he who noticed that a small sandstone block had been carved. And what a carving!

If, when I was finishing that earlier book, someone had told me that we would soon have an image of a Silurian warrior in our hands, I would have been more than a little sceptical. I think I would have said it was a terrific idea but I wouldn't hold my breath.

What the carving showed, however, was the image of a man portrayed from the waist up. There was no apparent clothing and a convincing argument can be made that his hands were bound behind him. The slightly vacant 'almond-shaped' eyes can be seen as Classical shorthand for a barbarian, a Celt.

There are other important elements. We have several Roman references to Celtic people noting a preference for long, drooping moustaches. Tacitus made a point of the 'curling hair' of the Silures. The image from the Priory Field has both, giving him an uncanny resemblance to the representation of a Silurian warrior used by the National Museum of Wales in its pre-millennium Celts in Wales exhibition.

The carving, now in the National Roman Legion Museum in Caerleon, is presented as a 'captured native'. That's OK; it's a safe description. However, as I explained at the outset, in this book I'm not being overly concerned about academic conventions so I'm inclined to go a bit further than that.

Let's remind ourselves that the Roman army had been engaged in a hard-fought quarter-century-long guerrilla war against the Silures. The legion had established itself in Isca/Caerleon to control the territory of the Silures. The Romans delighted in portraying captured enemies; examples abound from Trajan's column in Rome to points throughout the empire.

I think we are on reasonably safe ground in drawing what seems to me to be a pretty obvious conclusion. For the first time in a very long time, indeed if ever before, we are able to look at an image and say with some confidence that we are looking at a representation of a captured Silurian warrior.

My dead Roman

One of the saddest recent developments in higher education in Wales is the closure of the university campus in Caerleon. The victim of a merger, it disappeared taking a very good department of history and archaeology with it. My next example, however, harks back to the heady days of growth and expansion that included construction of a new, well-equipped sports centre in 1995.

Work digging foundations for a large new building followed on from an archaeological assessment, which had not suggested there would be much of interest. There was, as a consequence, some surprise when the large machine sliced through a Roman bath stone coffin.

Meeting the Silures? The image found in recent excavations in Caerleon. It is now displayed in the National Roman Legion Museum as the 'captured native' and, as is usually the case, there are a number of interpretations. To my mind, it's a captured Silurian warrior. (National Museum of Wales)

The bucket of the machine cut through at about shoulder level, tossing the lower portion of the coffin and its contents onto the spoil tip. I'm told on good authority that the supervisor, thinking that they had cut an old field drain, stopped the machine. He then climbed into the now rather large hole, reached into the 'field drain', pulled out a skull, said 'Bloody hell' and put it back!

The contractors then called the police.

That was exciting for a little while. There were patrol cars, sirens, flashing blue lights and a rapidly cordoned off site. I think their visit lasted about twenty minutes. They then informed the university authorities that 'we think this one is a bit old for us' and left.

That was the point at which the phone on my desk rang. I was able to assemble a team of students quite quickly, Susan Fox came up from the museum, and we started trying to recover what we could.

In the event, I think we did pretty well with what had, with a single swipe of the machine's bucket, become a very disturbed site. Time was a factor and the weather conditions were appalling, as is often the case with rescue archaeology. The monsoon conditions were bad enough that when Susan and I climbed in to try to retrieve what was left *in situ* ourselves, at one point she suggested to me that 'If we don't hurry up, there are going to be three bodies in here.' I could see what she meant.

By the time we had finished, we had recovered almost all of the coffin fragments and most of the skeleton as well as a small glass vessel, presumably a scent bottle, and a shale bowl. We saved enough that it was to become one of the main exhibits in the National Roman Legion Museum, where it remains to this day. When you enter the museum today, there on your right, in pride of place, are the remains of what I still think of as 'my dead Roman'.

Of course, that is pleasing but initially it was also a bit frustrating because skeletal material can tell you a great deal. That is it can if you are able to find sufficient funds to do the necessary investigations and initially neither we nor the museum had the resources.

This is the point at which the hard work of Mark Lewis, whom you have met before, and Dai Price, the museum manager, bore fruit. A funding package was eventually put in place and our Roman began to reveal his secrets.

To begin with, radiocarbon dating told us that this man, roughly 40 years old, had been buried in the late second or early third century. In other words, it was well over a hundred years after the foundation of the fortress when he died. The fact that he had been placed in what must have been an expensive coffin with grave goods suggests that he was someone of status, someone important in the fortress. A senior officer or an important contractor seem good possibilities.

Whatever the case, the prospect of finding out where this man had come from was tantalising. We have talked about movement of peoples within the empire and about the nature of populations in south-east Wales at various points in this book. Here was an opportunity to add to our knowledge on this question. Was our high-status individual from Rome? Could he have grown up in Gaul, or Spain, or northern Africa?

Happily, there is a good way to find out – measure the strontium levels, particularly in his teeth. As you have seen, however, it took a while to find funding so we had to wait to find out. At least the delay allowed for plenty of speculation.

Now, happily, we know. The answer came as a surprise to many people – he was local. Our Roman had grown up somewhere in or near Caerleon/Caerwent.

The fact that our high-status individual was a local man is interesting. It doesn't, of course, mean that he was a descendent of the Silures. But given my interests, you can imagine the way my mind was working. With the passing of time, the Romans often recruited locals from conquered lands and an association with the army might have been appealing for someone with Silurian antecedents. We can't say that he was. But he might have been!

Wing forward?

That still left another piece of the jigsaw to come. Funding had provided for a facial reconstruction and I was keen to 'meet' my Roman. I felt a sort of bond after our efforts to recover him. That's probably why I was so excited by the prospect of meeting him 'face to face'.

Facial reconstruction is a meticulous and time-consuming business so, once again, it took time. Now, at this point you may think I'm losing the plot and drifting right off the point. But stay with me, you'll see where I'm going with this shortly.

First, let me explain that I have interests other than history and archaeology. Through the years, rugby has been one of them. On the day in question, I had actually spent the best part of the afternoon on the university pitch, registering players with the WRU (Welsh Rugby Union). Getting rugby players to fill in forms correctly can sometimes be on the challenging side. The process took a little longer than I had hoped.

When I finally arrived home, slightly later than planned, there was an email from Mark saying that the reconstruction had been completed and an image was attached. I hurriedly opened the attachment and, at last, 'met' my dead Roman. I'm not telling you this for dramatic effect or trying to embellish the story. My immediate reaction was 'Crikey – I've just been talking to him this afternoon!'

In time, the museum refined its display. One of their strategies was to age and Romanise the reconstruction, which is fair enough. The reconstruction was that of a young man and our Roman had been moving into middle age. That is how the museum chose to represent him.

I couldn't, however, get the possible Silurian connection out of my mind. So, I turned to my son and daughter-in-law, who have good computer skills. The challenge was to say what if our chap took after his great-, great-, great-, etc. grandfather. Could we play with the image and put him in the forest for a few weeks watching and waiting for passing Romans? What would he look like if we did?

Well, you can see the result and I'm quite pleased with it. It's true that there is a striking resemblance to one of the current Wales second rows, which is probably entirely coincidental. Or possibly not!

Much as I would like to, I can't point to the Priory Field image or to our facial reconstruction and say, hand on heart, you've now come face to face with the Silures. However, I think we've come closer now than I would have thought possible only a few years ago.

So, let's leave it there for now and turn our thoughts toward how to understand the social structures of these people a little better.

'My dead Roman': the facial reconstruction from the Roman inhumation recovered on the university campus site. Accompanying is the imaginative 'Silurification' of the image discussed in the text. (Facial depiction by Professor Caroline Wilkinson, courtesy of the University of Dundee)

Derived 'native image'. (David and Hannah Howell)

12

Clans and clusters:
A research strategy

I almost called this book something like *Silures: Structures of society*. At the end of the day, however, I decided that sounded a bit stuffy and perhaps a little boring. I actually find it quite exciting because trying to unravel the structure or structures of their society is certainly key to improving our understanding of these people.

As we have discussed throughout the book, our evidence base is patchy. Moreover, there is a certain tension in interpreting the artefact assemblages that we have. Some things seem to point to considerable social cohesion across the area, while others suggest quite a lot of regional variation. Finding some sort of sensible balance inevitably becomes a prime objective.

One of the problems emerged in a television programme I was involved in not so long ago. As I've explained, I quite like participating in a programme now and again and *Time Team* provided a particularly entertaining break from the everyday academic routine. It was, however, always a fairly intense three days on site. When you do five takes of everything from various camera angles, it can become a little repetitive for the participants.

One of the interesting things about taking so many shots of all manner of things is that it means you're never sure what will or won't actually go out in the final, edited version. A classic case in point came in the Caerau hillfort programme, which I've told you a bit about already. In this one, almost everything I was involved with was actually broadcast. What I want to think about here is the bit that wasn't.

From the early planning stage, the programme makers had come up with a 'hook' for the episode. Basically, Caerau in Ely is effectively Cardiff – Cardiff is now the capital of Wales – the hillfort is a big and imposing one – we can present it as an Iron Age Welsh capital. We've seen how important the site is and discussed ways in which ongoing investigations there have already contributed significantly to our understanding. That's not the same thing as equating the site with a modern capital.

The excavation was directed by Oliver Davis and Niall Sharples of Cardiff University. Niall Sharples has established a well-earned position as one of Britain's leading late prehistorians. The filming sequence I have been alluding to is me and Niall trying to explain to Tony Robinson why the theme of an Iron Age capital might not be a very good idea. That didn't fit in with the plan so I'm afraid it was onto the cutting-room floor. The reason we thought it wasn't a particularly good idea is that it fails to take into account significant regional diversity and, as a consequence, is probably not the best explanation for the structure of Iron Age society in the region.

So, what is?

When I wrote the first book on Silures, I pitched the idea of clan-based confederation as a working model. In the interim, I've refined my thinking a bit but I still think that this is a pretty good bet.

Let me summarise the way I was thinking in 2013 and in doing so make mention of what I continue to think was a missed opportunity. By that year, as well as being professor I was also, among other things, director of a research group styled the South Wales Centre for Historical and Interdisciplinary Research. That sounds an unnecessarily convoluted name but we were enmeshed in the tentacles of merger by then and needed to broaden our appeal as widely as we could. You could see the process in the latest rebranding of our department as Heritage, Archaeology and Historical Studies.

You may have guessed that by this time I was possibly a little obsessed with Silures and I managed to scrape together enough money for a small publication called *Silurian Studies, Occasional Papers 1*. It's clear that the intention was to follow with 2, 3, etc. Unfortunately, that isn't going to happen now but if you do happen to have a copy, I would hold onto it. Novelty value might be worth something one day.

If you read it, you'll find an article by Giles Oatley and me called 'GIS Viewsheds and Social Network Analysis Interpretation of Iron Age Hillforts in South-East Wales'. That was a mouthful of a title but it does tell you exactly what the article was about. There was also an interesting piece by postgraduate student Siân Charlton about ritual deposition among the Silures and one by David, my son, who had joined the staff while finishing his PhD, about Celts and national heritage strategies.

I wrote an introduction in which I explained a bit about what we meant by 'Silurian Studies' and produced a brief introduction to the articles, including our viewshed study. The thinking then pretty much reflects my thinking now. I suggested that 'the approach recommends itself as a way to improve our understanding at a time when financial and other constraints limit opportunities for excavation'.

I went on to suggest that 'preliminary results are encouraging as application of this type of analysis demonstrates interesting relationships between hillforts with respect to both clustering and line-of-sight communication. As a consequence, it may also provide clues to important aspects of the social structure in the study area during the Iron Age.'

That still sounds about right to me.

So, what should we do now? How can we further our understanding of these Iron Age communities within the various constraints that are inevitable at the moment? Here are a few ideas that might be helpful.

Space and place

Among the findings of the occasional paper and other articles that we produced were a number of interesting spatial relationships. I think that Giles and I have now clearly demonstrated, at least to our own satisfaction, line-of-site communication; in south-east Wales you won't find a hillfort from which you can't see at least one other hillfort. You might find this persuasive in suggesting a degree of interaction over distances.

On the other hand, we're also confident that we are seeing clustering of hillforts that may suggest a tighter geographical focus. This seems to reflect some of the artefactual evidence that we have. Remember the apparent variation in ceramics but close association of metalwork that we have discussed.

The main point, I think, is that exploring these spatial relationships offers a way to expand our understanding. The idea has an increasing number of adherents and we all know what some of the limitations are. One of the big ones is the issue of dating. Without an extensive excavation programme, we have no dating for many of these sites. We cannot even be sure that sites in proximity were occupied at the same time or if there were changes in use over time.

The fact that we are usually unable to say whether hillfort A was contemporary with hillfort B is a problem. It's such a problem that there are some who say it's not worth doing comparisons until that information is to hand. I think that this chicken-and-egg conundrum leaves us in limbo unnecessarily.

Whatever the sequencing is, at least we know that, with one or two possible exceptions, all these sites were features in the landscape at the time the Romans invaded. The spatial relationships are of interest whatever the dating sequence might prove to be. Very little funding is available for excavation so let's not ignore a body of evidence for the next fifty years or so just because our data sets are incomplete. Clearly, from the outset we must acknowledge the weaknesses arising from this and other problems associated with the approach, but let's press on with the research and see where it takes us.

At this point, I'd like to note the contribution of Jerrad Lancaster. He had read our, and other, studies and decided to do exactly what I've just recommended to you – press on with the research and see where it takes us.

I was the external examiner on a spatial relationship study that he undertook. What pleased and impressed me was that he was brave enough to start drawing circles on the map. I was so pleased to see hillfort clusters in south-east Wales being presented in this way, that I was delighted to be able, in my role as 'Art and Archaeology Editor' of the journal *Studia Celtica*, to publish a version in the journal shortly thereafter.

Now I think we need to take things further and start drilling into possible clusters. There are obvious things that we should look at like clustering, orientation and nature of entrances, vallation, etc. We also need to try to contextualise sites in their landscape.

I'll give you an example of contextualising that I think about quite often. In fact, I suppose I think about it just about every day because the landscape in question lies spread out below me through the kitchen window. The valley extends east and west with the Gaer Fawr hillfort in clear site on the high ground opposite.

There are earthworks up behind the house, and if you drive down the hill a bit you come to the Great House hillfort. In the notes that follow, I say that I tend to think of Gaer Fawr and Great House as 'working in concert'. What I mean by that is that the valley is fertile farming land today and there is every reason to assume that it was fertile farm land in the Iron Age.

The two hillforts dominate the ridges controlling the entrance to the valley. The earthworks above are well placed to keep an eye on the top of the valley. An obvious conclusion is that the hillforts control the agricultural production. I think that makes sense in this particular case and that it provides a good working model for similar arrangements throughout south-east Wales.

Mapping and a 'few boots on the ground'

So, what shall we do now? For a start, I think we should have a good look at some of the very tantalising sites that Toby Driver has identified from the air. In particular, I would like to see a bit of survey on the apparent marching camps. These seem to be providing us with graphic physical evidence of the Silurian War so they are well worth a bit of fieldwork. Similarly, I'm fascinated by Toby's images from the Wyndcliff. This apparent Iron Age/Romano-British complex demands our attention and clearly justifies further investigation.

A good way to begin some potentially very exciting fieldwork is, I think, to involve local societies with a view to deploying interested local people on these sites to have a look. Obvious candidates to take the lead in this are Chepstow

Archaeological Society and the Monmouthshire Antiquarian Association. As luck would have it, at the moment I'm president of the first and chairman of the second so well placed to try to get the ball rolling.

With that objective in mind, just before the onset of the pandemic and the first lockdown, a few of us met with Toby for a chat over dinner in Cardiff and subsequently started to organise things. Then the pandemic hit!

As I write this, we are still in lockdown, making fieldwork difficult if not impossible at the moment. However, these problems will end and this initiative will, I'm confident, re-emerge high on the to-do list for all of us.

Annoyingly, another research initiative has also been put on hold. Giles is interested in continuing our investigations and I have recently met Simon Maddison, who has published some very useful work on hillforts in different parts of Britain. We decided that a three-way collaboration could pay dividends and were beginning to put together a research design.

We identified possible clusters (my early working model follows in the Appendix) and selected good groupings to target. Part of the process would be overflying sites with drones to help improve our understanding. We were just about on the launch pad when the pandemic struck, putting everything on hold. We hope to resume in due course.

I hope that this 'things are on hold' doesn't put you off. It would be nice to be able to finish the book with a comprehensive summary of Silurian society. However, as you now know there isn't one yet. Happily, things are improving, even if more slowly than we would like; we know more about the Silures now than we did when I wrote the first book.

As a consequence, we can press on and improve the picture even more. If this sounds insular, it doesn't need to be. There are hillfort studies waiting to be undertaken through the length and breadth of Britain and beyond. Even if you don't have local hillforts where you live, there are almost always ways to engage with the story of 'early people' in any area.

As for south-east Wales, the land of the Silures, I'm optimistic that these cluster studies and other investigations will pay dividends. As we improve our knowledge base, there are other things I'd like to look at. One example is a comparison between our cluster models and the early medieval landscape.

We have discussed the complex picture that emerges from historical studies of the possibly stylised but reasonably well documented system of trefi, cantrefi and other land divisions found in early medieval Wales. I'm curious how closely these might fit with revised and expanded cluster models. Is there any replication of Iron Age organisation in the post-Roman, pre-Norman period? Geographical determinism should still have been at work – I think it will be interesting to have a look.

I am increasingly convinced that clustering arising from a clan-based confederal structure will prove to be at the heart of the world of the Silures. I even have an image of sorts in mind and am happy to share it with you.

At this point, you may think I'm going off the rails a bit, but give it some thought. I've told you already that rugby has been quite an important diversion for me. Over the years, I have played, coached and finally found myself on several WRU committees. It's that last bit that started me thinking. I sometimes tell groups to whom I've been invited to speak that I like to think of the Silures in the context of the Welsh Rugby Union. They usually think I'm joking. I'm not!

Here is an example of a competitive society that requires a confrontational mindset. The most fiercely contested fixtures are frequently the local derbies. You want to beat the next village, the closest town, the neighbouring region. However, introduce an external threat like a team from over the border or a touring party and things can quickly become very focused in providing a united front. I don't want to be seen as trivialising things by comparing our game, however seriously we take it, to the life and death struggle of the Silures but I'll bet you can see the point. A white jersey with a rose on may not have quite the same effect as a Roman standard and armour. But then again, it might not be such a bad analogy!

Let's try to put all that in a slightly more 'academic' way. I tend to see south-east Wales as a common cultural zone. There must have been significant regional variation. However, there was also commonality of culture, tradition and language. There were also interactions seen in aspects of material culture probably reinforced by kin groups. A close confederation of clans reflected in things like hillfort clusters seems a good model.

It's perfectly possible to have a regional focus that can quickly coalesce into a united front. Increasingly, I think that might well have been the case with our Iron Age people. Tribes and sub-tribes, clusters and clans, can mass sufficiently to conduct a resistance like that seen in the Silurian War.

Conclusion

The Silures present us with a fascinating story of a determined and sophisticated Iron Age people. They would linger in the memory and demand our attention just on the basis of the remarkable resistance that they mounted in the quarter-century-long Silurian War.

As we have seen through this book, however, there is much more. Their social organisation isn't well enough understood but what we do know is tantalising. Their material culture was impressive, especially the intricately artistic La Tène-inspired metalwork.

Particularly interesting, and I think particularly important, is the predominance of equestrian equipment in this metalwork. The impressive array of items like terrets confirms the use of wheeled vehicles and, as I've suggested to you, items like the Lesser Garth terret seem to me to shout 'chariots' and 'equestrian elite'.

I said at the beginning of the last chapter that I had mused on the subtitle for the book. In the end, resistance, resilience and revival struck a chord with me. It wasn't simply a case of 'three Rs', looking good on the cover. I think they provide a pretty sound framework.

Resistance is obvious. The Silurian War was remarkable and you simply have to remind yourself of the fact that the Silures defeated a legion to emphasise the point.

Resilience also seems appropriate. It took time, but the tribal identity and presumably associated structures survived sufficiently intact to function as a civitas. I think this re-assertion of tribal identity is a key feature of Venta/Caerwent. The Paulinus stone and other bits of evidence speak of resilience.

I, along with many other people, enjoy a song written by Dafydd Iwan. It has become an anthem of sorts and has a particular resonance with someone who has spent a few decades teaching Welsh history and archaeology. The chorus ends 'er gwaetha pawb a phopeth, ry'n ni yma o hyd' – in spite of everyone and everything, we're still here! That sums things up nicely, I think.

And, what about revival? In the future, we want to look at things like landscape continuity and possible surviving traditions and organisational structures, but to a large extent the revival bit is down to us. There is work to be done and in the Appendix, I suggest one of the ways in which I think we can begin to do it. So, let's press on and see how much more of the story of the Silures we can revive. It's a task worth undertaking.

Let's finish with another story.

Back in the days of university mergers, we were earning money any way we could (within reason, of course). One avenue was to produce our own educational videos and we made what I thought was a good one on Caerleon.

The story of Isca was a bilingual production; shoot one scene in Welsh and then shoot it again in English. As luck would have it, Iestyn Jones was on the scene finishing his PhD and he already had a distinguished acting career on S4C (Sianel Pedwar Cymru – the Welsh-language channel). He was happy to be involved and became our presenter.

The idea was that Iestyn would dress in accurate reproduction armour from the museum and present the programmes from various locations, kitted out as a Roman centurion. We identified various sites for filming and extended our remit to take in places like Lodge Hill. When we filmed at the hillfort, we had Iestyn on top of the large inner rampart explaining about the site, the Silurian War, etc.

As we were filming, who should come striding into the hillfort but a youngish lad walking no fewer than five dogs on leads. He strode past – stopped short (you don't see all that many centurions about these days) – turned around and asked 'You lot aren't coming back, are you?' He walked on, but only for a couple of paces. He then stopped and turned around again, saying 'We'll bloody have you next time!' before striding away.

That made my day. He was clearly aware of the Celt/Roman narrative and I can't help thinking that the belligerent tone would have found favour with the Silures who once lived in the hillfort.

Yma o hyd, indeed.

Notes and further reading

As I explained at the outset, I'm approaching this book differently from my earlier efforts. This is particularly the case with the notes, which I want to be useful without becoming tedious and/or distracting. I'll simply point you towards some additional reading and useful sources of information rather than trying to cite every reference, chapter and verse. I hope that you will find this a user-friendly approach. Some colleagues and students may find it a bit annoying, but they will be well versed in the idea of going to other sources and following references. Hopefully, everyone will cope.

Chapter 1

As background to the introduction to the book and the subject, there is some general reading that you may want to consider. It might seem bad form to recommend my own books; but, then again, you may want to have a look. My first book about the Silures is still in print and while it offers less up-to-the-minute information it is pretty thorough with things like artefact reviews, etc. It's *Searching for the Silures: An Iron Age Tribe in South-East Wales* (The History Press, 2009).

There are some other admittedly self-interested recommendations you might want to consider. In due course, you will be introduced to my friend and colleague Miranda Aldhouse-Green, a leading authority on early, particularly Iron Age, religion. She and I have collaborated on several projects but there are two books to mention at this stage. The first is a small volume called *Celtic Wales*. She and I are the co-authors of this overview published by University of Wales Press, first in 2000 and subsequently in 2017.

We also co-edited the first volume of the Gwent County History. This is a particular recommendation because we assembled leading authorities to contribute chapters including Adam Gwilt and Mike Hamilton on aspects of the Bronze Age, and Richard Brewer and Bill Manning on Roman Gwent. Miranda wrote a chapter on 'Art, Ritual and Society', Josh Pollard and I on the Iron Age and I produced a chapter on the fifth to seventh centuries. If you want to pursue things more fully, this, I think, is well worth reading. So, here it is in full: Aldhouse-Green, M. and Howell, R. (eds.), *The Gwent County*

History Volume 1, Gwent in Prehistory and Early History (University of Wales Press, 2004). There are also several important things by Adam Gwilt, the Principal Curator: Prehistory in the National Museum of Wales, which you might like to read. In due course, I'll be referring you to reports on the excavations at Llanmaes including important publications from 2011 and 2015. For now, you might want to have a look at the volume that he co-edited, with Colin Hazelgrove, *Reconstructing Iron Age Societies* (Oxbow Monographs, 1997) and his 'Silent Silures: Locating People and Places in the Iron Age of South Wales' in Haselgrove, C. and Moore, T. (eds.), *The Later Iron Age in Britain and Beyond* Oxbow (2007).

Rounding off good introductory sources that you will find helpful is Barry Cunliffe's *Iron Age Communities in Britain*. Barry Cunliffe is the widely respected 'doyen' of British Iron Age studies. As we proceed, I will be recommending a number of his publications including one or two 'hot off the press'. *Iron Age Communities*, first published in 1971 by Routledge, remains the obvious starting place for someone wanting to begin to understand the British Iron Age. The fourth edition appeared in 2009.

Throughout this book, I refer to matters like tribal identity. It's worth noting that use of the term 'tribe' can become problematic for some commentators. Here, as with other themes in the text, it's important to define our terms. Tribes throughout the world, in many different periods, take many forms. The term need not imply hierarchical social structures or high degrees of organisation and control. I prefer to think in terms of common cultural zones, often in large part defined by language, culture and familial relationships. If regional identity sits more comfortably with you, go for it. I'll stick with tribal.

A final thought – the story of the Silures is an important element in the early history of Wales. A good historical overview with a useful prehistory section is *Hanes Cymru* by John Davies, which appeared in 1990 (Allen Lane, The Penguin Press). This history of the country, written in Welsh, was then translated into English by the author and, as *A History of Wales*, published in 1993. A 2007 edition of both is available. It's worth a read.

Chapter 2

To read further on the subject matter of this chapter, the obvious starting point is the books of Tacitus. There are a number of translations available; Penguin Classics is a good choice. The three books that specifically mention the Silures are available in the Classics series: *The Histories*, trans. Ash, R. and Wellesley, K. (2009); *The Annals*, trans. Grant, M. (2003); and *The Agricola*, trans. Mattingly, H. (2010).

Translations will always result in different nuances and, at times, disagreement about meaning. In chapters to come, I'll be recommending a look at the Latin in places. You might find that interesting anyway. Just a word of warning – if you're armed with your Latin dictionary and decide to move on from Tacitus, don't be overly surprised when you have a go at Cassius Dio. He wrote in Greek! A case in point is the translation I've given you in the text with respect to Caratacus and his observations on Rome. The comparison is usually translated 'huts'. For reasons we will consider in more depth in the text, this is a poor choice. I've given you 'roundhouses', which I think is better.

Tacitus will provide an interesting context with plenty of background on Rome. You might also like to be able to refer to a good general historical overview. For Roman Britain, an obvious starting point is Peter Salway's *Roman Britain* in the annoyingly named Oxford History of England series. He does actually write about Wales! For a concise version, you could try his *Roman Britain: A Very Short Introduction*, also published by Oxford University Press (2015).

For inscriptions, the first port of call is generally Collingwood, R. and Wright, R., *Roman Inscriptions of Britain* (Oxford University Press). First published in 1965, there is now an up-to-date digitally enhanced version readily available online at https://romanin-scriptionsofbritain.org/.

For the particular examples discussed in the text, you might want to start with Richard Brewer's volume *Corpus Signorum Imperii: Corpus of Sculpture of the Roman World*, Vol. I Fascicule 5 (British Academy and Oxford University Press, 1986). You will probably also want to consult Tomlin, R., *Britannia Romana: Roman Inscriptions and Roman Britain* (Oxbow, 2017).

For a concise description of inscriptions mentioned in the text, the well-illustrated Cadw guides to Caerwent and Caerleon, available in Welsh and English, are useful. You will have noticed that I'm giving you measurements in imperial and metric. Long ago, I recognised that things like excavation reports must now be metric so that's how I do measurements on site. When I'm up in the woods planting, clearing, etc. on Brynheulog, however, I find I still use and think in imperial and measure accordingly. You might be the same. Besides, it doesn't hurt to have both!

The Caerwent inscriptions are considered in several chapters of the *County History* and by Bill Manning in his book *Roman Wales* (University of Wales Press, 2001). Thoughts on the Goldcliff Stone can be found in Knight, J., 'The Goldcliff Stone: A Reconsideration', in *The Monmouthshire Antiquary*, 1/2 (1962) and in Mason, D., '*Prata Legionis* in Britain', in *Britannia*, 19 (1988).

For evidence of conflation of religions and the influences reflected in the dedications discussed in this chapter you will want to turn to Miranda Aldhouse-Green. Start with the *County History* and go from there. Conversely, you could jump to the notes accompanying the chapter on religion where I will be giving you a more detailed choice of sources, many of them by Miranda.

That's probably enough to be getting on with for now. Before we leave a consideration of the historical scene, however, there is another point worth mentioning. In 1985, HTV Wales (as it was then) produced a major series called *The Dragon Has Two Tongues* with Gwyn Alf Williams and Wynford Vaughan Thomas as presenters. They both also produced histories of Wales – *When Was Wales* by Gwyn Alf and *Wales, a History* by Wynford Vaughan Thomas. The idea was that the latter would offer a conventional for the time, traditional interpretation while Gwyn Alf would bring his fiery Marxist approach to the study. These were interesting books and the series was a fascinating exercise for television.

If nothing else, the series confirmed how two serious and well-informed people can look at the same place, over the same period, drawing on the same evidence, and reach very different conclusions. It's a good lesson to keep in mind when we consider the history of the Silures or, indeed, anything else.

Chapter 3

If you want to pursue the late Bronze Age/early Iron Age transition in more depth, I would recommend starting with the *County History*. For the axes in particular, read Adam Gwilt's chapter 'Late Bronze Age Societies (1150–600 BC): Tools and Weapons'.

For hillforts, there is a risk of overload and I will be providing you with a more comprehensive list when we reach Chapter 7. For now, keep things that I've already recommended to you, like *Iron Age Communities* and the chapter Josh and I wrote for the *County History*, in mind. From there, everyone's starting point is the *Atlas*.

A major contribution to Iron Age studies is Lock, G. and Ralston, I., *Atlas of Hillforts of Britain and Ireland* (Edinburgh University Press, 2021). This compendium is available online and is now a first port of call for hillfort studies (hillforts.arch.ox.ac.uk).

You might also find an earlier study of interest. If so, have a look at Guilbert, G. (ed.) *Hill-fort Studies: Essays for A.H.A.Hogg* (Leicester University Press, 1981).

The Caerau excavations that are mentioned in this chapter are of particular importance to anyone interested in the Iron Age in south Wales. The subject will return in later chapters. To bring yourself up to date on this ongoing investigation, have a look at Davis, O. and Sharples, N., *Excavations at Caerau Hillfort, Cardiff, South Wales, 2015, an Interim Report*, Cardiff Studies in Archaeology - Specialist Report No. 36 (Department of Archaeology and Conservation, Cardiff University, 2016).

Also important is Davis, O. and Sharples, N. 'Excavations at Caerau Hillfort, Cardiff: Towards a Narrative for the Hillforts of South-East Wales', a published paper for an international colloquium on *Late Prehistoric Fortifications in Europe: Defensive, Symbolic and Territorial Aspects from the Chalcolithic to the Iron Age* (Archaeopress, 2020). This not only updates the reader on progress but also examines aspects of particular matters of interest like hillfort clusters in Glamorgan.

By this stage you will have a number of recommended sources by Niall Sharples. You would probably like to add important earlier studies such as *Maiden Castle Excavations and field survey 1985–6* (English Heritage Archaeological Report 19, 1991) and *Social Relations in Later Prehistory: Wessex in the First Millennium* BC (Oxford University Press, 2010).

For the ritual deposits, I would recommend starting with Miranda; it's worth reading her thoughts both in the *County History* and in our book *Celtic Wales* (2017). You might also enjoy some useful earlier accounts, particularly those of Hubert Savory like *Guide Catalogue of the Early Iron Age Collections* (National Museum of Wales, 1976) and 'Early Iron Age Glamorgan' in the *Glamorgan County History*, Volume II, which he edited (1984).

There are good discussions of La Tène and Hallstatt in the general sources recommended above but you might also be interested in having a look at things like Ruth and Vincent Megaw's now classic *Celtic Art: From its Beginnings to the Book of* Kells (2001) and Miranda's *Celtic Art: Reading the Messages* (1996) and *Celtic Art: Symbols and Imagery* (1997).

A useful overview which you will find helpful is Lynch, F., Aldhouse-Green, S. and Davies, J. *Prehistoric Wales* (Sutton, 2000). There is a wealth of material on artefact assemblages and I don't want to swamp you but it is worth consulting Boon, G. and Lewis, J. (eds.) *Welsh Antiquity* (National Museum of Wales, 1976) especially entries like Davies, J. and Spratling, M. 'The Seven Sisters Hoard: A Centenary Study'. You may also find Aldhouse-Green, M. and Webster, P. (eds.) *Artefacts and Archaeology: Aspects of the Celtic and Roman World* (University of Wales Press, 2002) useful.

On the issue of lost/missing items like the helmets, you can start with a bit of antiquarian research and look at Francis, G. 'On Ancient Bronze Helmets Found in 1818 at Ogmore Down, Glamorganshire', in *Archaeologia*, 43 (1871–2). A more recent discussion is Toft, L. 'The Nineteenth-Century Discovery and Loss of the "Ogmore Helmets"', in *Archaeologia Cambrensis*, 147 (1998).

In the main, detailed ceramic and metalwork descriptions form part of excavation reports so this might be a good time to introduce you to some key ones. With respect to Llanmelin, for example, the 1930s report is Nash-Williams, V. 'An Early Iron Age Hill-fort at Llanmelin, near Caerwent, Monmouthshire', in *Archaeologia Cambrensis*, 88 (1933).

More recent Cadw investigations can be found in Pannett, A. and Pudney, C. 'Llanmelin Hillfort Excavations', Cadw Assessment Report (2013) – you can go online at cadw.gov. wales/about/projects-researchprojects/Llanmelin-wood-hillfort-excavations. Of interest might also be Pudney, C. 'A Bone-Disc Nail Cleaner from South-East Wales', in *The Monmouthshire Antiquary*, 33 (2017).

The slightly later excavation of the Sudbrook promontory fort is Nash-Williams, V. 'An Early Iron Age Coastal Camp at Sudbrook', in *Archaeologia Cambrensis*, 94 (1939). For a summary of the more recent investigations, have a look at Sell, S., Gwilt, A. and Webster, P. 'Recent Excavation and Survey Work at Sudbrook Camp, Portskewett, Monmouthsire' (ST 507 873), *Studia Celtica*, 35 (2001).

For Lodge Hill, Josh and I did a short report for *Archaeology in Wales*, 40 (2000). The excavation report is Pollard, J., Howell, R., Chadwick, A. and Leaver, A., *Lodge Hill Camp, Caerleon and the Hillforts of Gwent*, British Archaeological Reports, British Series 207 (2006).

For Gwent prehistoric sites, the first stopping point is usually Children, G. and Nash, G. *Prehistoric Sites of Monmouthshire* (Logaston, 1996).

Like excavations at Caerau, the Pembrokeshire chariot burial is a game-changer in terms of Welsh Iron Age studies. Updates, including an excavation blog, can be found on the National Museum of Wales website (museum.wales/blog/2058/Volunteer-Blog-The-Chariot-Project). Full reports will be appearing in due course.

Interestingly, work on this book was put on hold briefly during the autumn of 2020 when I became involved in preparation of a co-production for television about the chariot. It was being made for S4C, the Welsh-language channel, and the Discovery Channel.

It was good fun to meet with Iestyn, who was the presenter for S4C, and do a bit of filming on Llanmelin again. The finished programme, 'Cyfrinach y Bedd Celtaidd' was screened in June 2021 – my possibly idiosyncratic rugby analogy on the programme appears again, elsewhere in this book!

Chapter 4

With respect to roads, our excavation of the likely looking candidate near Lodge Hill is published as: Howell, R. 'An Investigation of Trackways on Park Farm near Caerleon', in *Archaeology in Wales*, 52 (2013).

For information on the Droitwich briquetage, have a look at the section by Josh and Elaine Morris in the Lodge Hill excavation report. For background you could try Morris, E. 'Prehistoric Salt Distributions: Two Case Studies from Western Britain', in *Bulletin of the Board of Celtic Studies*, 32 (1985); and Woodiwiss, S. (ed.) *Iron Age and Roman Salt Production and the Medieval Town of Droitwich*, CBA Research Report 81 (1992).

There are many discussions of Iron Age trade and trading systems in a number of the books I've already recommended to you. Another source that I have found to be useful is Macready, S. and Thompson, P. (eds.) *Cross-Channel Trade between Gaul and Britain in the Pre-Roman Iron Age* (Society of Antiquaries, 1984).

There is a wide choice for further reading about early ships and shipping. Once again, it's a good idea to start with Barry Cunliffe. His *Facing the Ocean* (Oxford University Press, 2001) is good but I would particularly recommend *On the Ocean* (Oxford

University Press, 2017). This is a really useful and interesting read. I found the orientation of the maps especially helpful. Have a look; you'll see what I mean.

The other obvious go-to source for early seafaring is Seán McGrail. There is a wide selection of books – here are a few to get you started. Roughly in sequence, you can work your way through *Ancient Boats in North-West Europe: The Archaeology of Water Transport to AD 1500* (1998); *Boats of the World: From the Stone Age to Medieval Times* (2002); *Early Ships and Seafaring: European Water Transport* (2014); and *Early Ships and Seafaring: Water Transport Beyond Europe* (2015). There is also *Ancient Boats and Ships* in the Shire Archaeology series (2006).

A particularly useful recent addition to this seafaring corpus examines the maritime history of Wales. You will want to have a look at this one. It's Redknap, M., Rees, S. and Aberg, A. (eds.) *Wales and the Sea: 10,000 Years of Welsh Maritime History*, published by Y Lolfa for the Royal Commission in partnership with the National Library, Cadw and the National Museum (2019).

I suspect that everyone working archaeologically in Wales should have a little note on the first page of their notebook saying something like 'If we find wet wood, call Nigel'. Nigel Nayling, professor at University of Wales Trinity Saint David, is the acknowledged wet wood specialist in Wales and beyond. Not surprisingly, that means he becomes involved with most 'boat-related' finds – which brings us nicely to the specific sites in south-east Wales mentioned in the text.

You will probably want to read Nayling, N., Maynard, D. and McGrail, S., 'Barlands Farm, Magor, Gwent: A Romano-British Boat Find' in *Antiquity*, 68 (1994) as well as Nayling, N. and McGrail, S. *The Barlands Farm Romano-Celtic Boat*, CBA Research Report 138 (2004).

Another to add to the list is Nayling, N. and Caseldine, A. *Excavations at Caldicot, Gwent: Bronze Age Palaeochannels in the Lower Nedern Valley,* CBA Research Report 108 (1997). If you want to pursue the issue of sewn boats, start with McGrail, S. and Kently, E. *Sewn Plank Boats,* British Archaeological Reports International Series 276 (1985).

With respect to coastal trade, creek ports, etc., Llanmaes is now the key site so have a look at Lodwick, M. and Gwilt, A. 'Concluding Seasons of Fieldwork at Llanmaes, Vale of Glamorgan 2009–2010', in *Archaeology in Wales*, 50 (2011) and Gwilt, A., Lodwick, M., Deacon, J., et al., 'Ephemeral Abundance at Llanmaes: Exploring the Residues and Resonances of an Earliest Iron Age Midden and its Associated Archaeological Context in the Vale of Glamorgan', in Koch, J. and Cunliffe, B. (eds.) *Celtic from the West, 3* (Oxbow, 2016). The three-volume compilation *Celtic from the West* represents a sea change in British Iron Age studies so we will be revisiting them shortly.

For a discussion of the coin of Caratacus, you can read Boon, G., 'A Coin of Caratacus in the National Museum of Wales', *Bulletin of the Board of Celtic Studies* (1973) and 'Further Observations on a Coin of Caratacus in the National Museum of Wales', *Bulletin of the Board of Celtic Studies* (1974).

Interestingly, as I was writing this in November 2020, press reports noted the sale of a golden coin showing an equestrian image of Caratacus, found by a metal detectorist near Newbury the year before. It sold for £71,000!

The reference to the Roman 'fortlets' at Old Burrow and Martinhoe comes from *Prehistoric Wales*, which I recommended to you in the notes to the previous chapter.

Chapter 5

The ironwork report on Lodge Hill was prepared by Phil Macdonald, with a separate report on the slag by Tim Young. Both are in the excavation report, which you are probably becoming quite familiar with by now. Things like quern stones are also best found in excavation reports and several relevant ones have already been recommended in the previous notes.

I don't want to become tedious here, but the best place to start on bones is also the various excavation reports. For example, have a look at Cowley, L. on the 'Osseus Remains' (1933) and on the 'Animal Remains' (1939) in the Llanmelin and Sudbrook reports respectively.

For the detailed English regional studies that I would very much like to see replicated in south-east Wales, look at Hambleton, E. *Animal Husbandry Regimes in Iron Age Britain: A Comparative Study of Faunal Assemblages from British Iron Age Sites,* British Archaeological Reports, British Series 282 (1999).

Miranda has a good descriptive account of the bull's head mount from Chepstow in the *County History*.

As we look to the Levels for insight relating to stock management, including the apparent rectangular byres, footprints and associated trackways, you could start with Martin Locock's 'Iron Age and Later Features at Greenmoor Arch (Gwent Europark), Newport', in *Archaeology in the Severn Estuary*, 10 (1999) and Locock, M. and Yates, A., 'Greenmoor Arch, Bishton (ST 400 866)', in *Archaeology in Wales*, 39 (1999).

It's worth making a note of *Archaeology in the Severn Estuary* as this is a very useful source on a range of issues. To streamline things, let's abbreviate it as *ASE* below. It will keep coming up. For good background, it is also well worth reading Rippon, S., *Gwent Levels: The Evolution of a Wetland Landscape*, CBA Research Report 105 (1996).

In the text I suggest that the Gwent Levels represent our best-understood prehistoric south-east Wales landscape. Much of that understanding is a consequence of the work of Martin Bell, professor of archaeological science at Reading, and his colleagues. So, let's have a look at aspects of that body of literature.

Sequentially, you may want to examine his 'Goldcliff Excavations 1991', *ASE* (1991); 'Field Survey and Excavation at Goldcliff 1992', *ASE* (1992); 'Field Survey and Excavation at Goldcliff, Gwent 1993', *ASE* (1993); 'Field Survey and Excavation at Goldcliff, Gwent 1994', *ASE* (1994).

You will also want to read Bell, M. and Neumann, H., 'Prehistoric Intertidal Archaeology and Environments in the Severn Estuary, Wales', in *World Archaeology* (1997) and Bell, M., Caseldine, A. and Neumann, H., *Prehistoric Intertidal Archaeology in the Welsh Severn Estuary*, CBA Research Report 120 (2000).

Martin's more recent publications include *Prehistoric Coastal Communities: The Mesolithic in Western Britain*, CBA Research Report 149 (2007) and *The Bronze Age in the Severn Estuary*, CBA Research Report 172 (2013). Hot off the press at the time of writing is *Making One's Way in the World: The Footprints and Trackways of Prehistoric People* (Oxbow, 2020).

Martin Bell's work has transformed our understanding and the results have been achieved in very difficult conditions. The sediments in the estuary produce remarkable preservation but the tides are daunting, limiting possible time on site and necessitating a major clean-up each day.

I've enjoyed visiting and continue to be impressed. However, don't try it on your own! Don't even contemplate going out onto the foreshore without someone very familiar with the area as your guide; make sure that that someone has carefully consulted the tide table. The conditions are challenging (that's a euphemism for dangerous). Mind you, if someone is very familiar with the area, it's a safe bet they will already have consulted the tide tables very carefully.

Chapter 6

When looking at roundhouses, there is an important point to note from the beginning: for many years it was fashionable to call these buildings 'huts'. In some cases, it still is – but it shouldn't be. There are pejorative connotations in the description and as I've explained in the text, well-made roundhouses can be comfortable and durable. Hut is OK to describe the structures some children like to build in the garden; these Iron Age buildings were roundhouses.

There is a wealth of published material about symbolic and other considerations that may have been important in roundhouse design. One example that we considered in the text was the orientation of entrances. If you want to read further, this might be a good place to start any background reading on the subject.

Consequently, you could begin with something like Oswald, A. 'A Doorway on the Past: Practical and Mystic Concerns on the Orientation of Roundhouse Doorways', in Gwilt, A. and Hazelgrove, C. (eds.) *Reconstructing Iron Age Societies* (Oxbow, 1997). Also worth reading is Parker Pearson, M., 'Food, Fertility and Front Doors in the First Millennium BC', in Champion, T. and Collis, J. (eds.) *The Iron Age in Britain and Ireland: Recent Trends* (University of Sheffield, 1996).

For an incisive analysis, I'd recommend Jones, I., *The Use of Social Space in Early Medieval Irish Houses with Particular Reference to Ulster*, BAR British Series 564 (2014). It may be largely Early Medieval and largely Irish but this is interesting and instructive.

For rectangular structures, I've already recommended our excavation report as well as publications about the buildings on the Levels. You might want to add to that list Moore, T., 'Rectangular Houses in the British Iron Age: "Squaring the Circle"', in Humphrey, J. (ed.) *Re-searching the Iron Age*, Leicester Archaeology Monographs 11 (2003).

There are references to surveys in the text. We will pick up some of those in the following chapter.

For reconstruction of roundhouses as an application of experimental archaeology, the starting point for most will be Butser Farm. Peter Reynolds was the driving force in the foundation of the site; it's well worth reading his descriptions of the project like *Iron-Age Farm: The Butser Experiment* (British Museum, 1976). His concise summary in the Shire series is *Ancient Farming* (1987). You may be inspired to visit. If you do, there is a guide: *Butser Ancient Farm Guide Book* (2009).

Hopefully you will also want to visit St Fagans. A good starting point for your visit to the reconstruction here is: Longley, D., 'Bryn Eryr: An Enclosed Settlement of the Iron Age on Anglesey', in *Proceedings of the Prehistoric Society*, 64 (2014).

Another site visit that I highly recommend to you is Castell Henllys near Eglwyswrw in Pembrokeshire. For background to this site, read Mytum, H., *Monumentality in Later Prehistory: Building and Rebuilding Castell Henllys Hillfort* (Springer, 2013).

A new and interesting account is Mytum, H. and Meek, J., 'Experimental Archaeology and Roundhouse Excavated Signatures: The Investigation of Two Reconstructed Iron Age Buildings at Castell Henllys', in *Archaeological and Anthropological Sciences*, 12 (2020).

Chapter 7

There is a large body of literature relating to hillforts. Remember the modern mantra that is that students of the subject should start with the *Atlas* and follow on from there.

For a flavour of the genre, you might also like to add to your list of sources by Barry Cunliffe his volume, co-edited with David Miles, *Aspects of the Iron Age in Central Southern Britain* (University of Oxford Committee for Archaeology, 1984). A must for serious students is also his six-volume report on excavations at Danebury, published from 1984. You might want to try these back to front, i.e. beginning with Vol. 6, *A Hillfort Community in Perspective* (1995). For a summary, you could go straight to his *Danebury Hillfort* (Tempus 2003).

For perspective with relation to developments in thinking over the years, you might find it interesting to look right back at something like Hawkes. C., 'Hill-forts' in *Antiquity* (1931). You could then move on to entries in Champion, T. and Collis, J., *The Iron Age in Britain and Ireland: Recent Trends* (1996), which was introduced in the notes to Chapter 6.

Following the references, you can work your way to more recent accounts that may include Ralston, I., *Celtic Fortifications* (The History Press, 2006) and Harding, D., *Iron Age Hillforts in Britain and Beyond* (University of Oxford, Committee for Archaeology, 2012). You will also want to refer to Sharples, N., *Social Relationships in Later Prehistory: Wessex in the First Millennium* BC (Oxford, 2010).

For Wales, Toby Driver has, in addition to his groundbreaking aerial investigations, made important specific contributions to hillfort studies. Have a look at *Architecture, Regional Identity and Power in the Iron Age Landscapes of Mid Wales: The Hillforts of North Ceredigion,* BAR British Series 583 (2013); *Hillforts of Cardigan Bay* (Logaston, 2016); and 'New Perspectives on the Architecture and Function of Welsh Hillforts and Defended Settlements', in *Internet Archaeology*, 48 (2018).

For more on aerial discoveries, try Driver, T., *Pembrokeshire Historic Landscapes from the Air,* RCAHMW (2007); and Driver, T., Burnham, B. and Davies, J., 'Roman Wales: Aerial Discoveries and New Observations from the Drought of 2018', in *Britannia*, 51 (2020).

Good recent contributions to our understanding within a part of the Silurian region have been made by Frank Olding, who has written *The Prehistoric Landscapes of the Eastern Black Mountains,* BAR British Series 297 (2000) and his bilingual Eisteddfod volume *Archaeoleg Ucheldir Gwent/Archaeology of Upland Gwent* (Royal Commission, 2016). In the latter, I should probably recommend the short contribution on Twm Barlwm (since I wrote it).

There are a number of sites where excavation and/or survey has been instructive. I've already recommended reports on Caerau, Llanmelin, Lodge Hill, Sudbrook and Twyn Y Gaer. Don't forget the Coed y Bwnydd site: Babbidge, A., 'Reconnaissance Excavations at Coed y Bwnydd, Betws Newydd, 1969–1979', in *Monmouthshire Antiquary*, 3 & 4 (1977). Also see Williams, D. 2006 'Llanmelin hillfort, Caerwent: geophysical and earthwork survey' in J. Pollard, R. Howell, A. Chadwick and A. Leaver *Lodge Hill Camp, Caerleon, and the Hillforts of Gwent*, British Archaeological Reports, British Series 407, Oxford: BAR Publishing. 62–7.

To explore further in Wales, you can consult the Royal Commission on the Ancient and Historical Monuments of Wales inventories for Glamorgan and the Commission's Brecknock inventory of prehistoric and Roman remains. You already know all about the *Gwent County History.*

There have been a number of excavations and surveys that you might want to consult if you are interested in specific sites. The easiest course here would simply be to refer you back to the *Atlas* with a suggestion to follow up the references. However, here are a few to get you started.

I tried to think of a way to group these in some sort of coherent and systematic way but couldn't. So here are some possibilities given in a random order. A good starting place might be Robinson, D. (ed.), *Biglis, Caldicot and Llandough*, BAR British Series 188 (1988). Specific entries in this one include Owen-John, H., 'Llandough: The Rescue Excavation of a Multi-period Site Near Cardiff, South Glamorgan'; Parkhouse, J., 'Excavations at Biglis, South Glamorgan'; and Vyner, B. and Allen, D., 'A Romano-British Settlement at Caldicot, Gwent'.

Henry Owen-John also investigated 'A Hill-Slope Enclosure in Coed y Cymdda, Near Wenvoe, South Glamorgan', in *Archaeologia Cambrensis* (1988). You may also be interested in Williams, A., 'Excavations at the Knave Promontory Fort, Rhossili, Glamorgan', *Archaeologia Cambrensis* (1939); 'The Excavation of Bishopston Valley Promontory Fort', *Archaeologia Cambrensis* (1940); and 'The Excavation of High Pennard Promontory Fort', *Archaeologia Cambrensis* (1941).

A more recent promontory fort excavation programme is that of Elizabeth Walker of the National Museum at the tidal island of Burry Holms, Gower. You could look at her 'Burry Holms (SS 4001 9247)', in *Archaeology in Wales* 41 (2001).

Jeff Davies has undertaken a number of important excavations, including 'Excavations at Cae Summerhouse, Tythegston, Glam.', in *Morgannwg*, 10 (1966); 'Excavations at Cae Summerhouse, Second Interim Report', in *Morgannwg*, 11 (1967); 'Excavations at Caer Dynnaf, Llanblethian, Glam. 1965–1967', in *Morgannwg*, 11 (1967); 'Bulwarks, Porthkerry', in *Archaeology in Wales*, 8 (1968); 'Cae Summerhouse, Tythegston', in *Archaeology in Wales*, 13 (1973); and 'An Excavation at the Bulwarks, Porthkerry, Glamorgan, 1968', in *Archaeologia Cambrensis*, 122 (1973).

As we've discussed in the text, some excavations were undertaken quite a long time ago. They can still tell us a thing or two; for example you could try Griffiths, J., 'Hen Dre'r Gelli: A Buried Prehistoric Town in the Rhondda Valley', in *Archaeologica Cambrensis*, 61 (1906). A bit more recent is Fox, C., 'Caer Dynnaf, Llanblethian: A Hillfort of Early Iron Age Type in the Vale of Glamorgan', in *Archaeologia Cambrensis* (1936). More modern investigations include Hogg, A., 'Castle Ditches, Llancarfan, Glamorgan', in *Archaeologia Cambrensis* (1976) and Morris, B., 'Llwynheirnin', in *Archaeology in Wales* (1968).

A site that I find particularly interesting in terms of the subject matter of this and subsequent chapters is reported by Gwilym Hughes. Have a look at his *The Excavation of a Late Prehistoric and Romano-British Settlement at Thornwell Farm, Chepstow, Gwent*, BAR British Series 168 (1996).

No doubt there are things I've missed out but that should be enough to be getting on with.

Chapter 8

We have already discussed further reading for aspects of religion, including the evidence for conflation of belief reflected in things like the inscriptions from Caerwent. Earlier I suggested that you start with Miranda on this topic and promised to provide a longer list of books that you might like to consult.

Here are several to add to your already fairly lengthy list; they are published by Thames and Hudson unless I tell you otherwise. A good starting point for both Iron Age religion and the issues of 'celticity' which we have looked at in the text is the *Dictionary of Celtic Myth and Legend* (1997). You could then move on to the book written with Stephen Aldhouse-Green, *The Quest for the Shaman: Shape-Shifters, Sorcerers, and Spirit-Healers of Ancient Europe* (2005); and *Boudica Britannia* (Taylor and Francis, 2006).

An important book for themes that we have considered in the text is *Exploring the World of the Druids* (2005). Another is *The Celtic Myths: A Guide to the Ancient Gods and Legends* (2008). You might also enjoy *Caesar's Druids: Story of an Ancient Priesthood* Yale (2010). More recent publications include *Bog Bodies Uncovered: Solving Europe's Ancient Mystery* (2015) and *Sacred Britannia: The Gods and Rituals of Roman Britain* (2018).

Moving on to the Celtic issue, the 'anti-Celt' pieces mentioned in the text are Collis, J. 'The Origin and Spread of the Celts', in *Studia Celtica*, 30 (1997); and James, S., *The Atlantic Celts: Ancient People or Modern Invention* (British Museum, 1999).

To advance the discussion and bring Wales into focus, you may want to have a look at some of the work of Raimund Karl, professor at Bangor. Try 'Random Coincidences? Or: The Return of the Celtic to Iron Age Britain', in *Proceedings of the Prehistoric Society*, 74 (2008); and 'Becoming Welsh: Modelling First Millennium BC Societies in Wales and the Celtic Context', in Moore, T. and Armada, L., *Atlantic Europe in the First Millennium BC: Crossing the Divide* (Oxford University Press, 2011). For a Welsh language take on things you could try Bowen, G. (gol.), *Y Gwareiddiad Celtaidd* (Gwasg Gomer, 1987).

I've suggested in the text that the real game-changers in this discussion are the three volumes of *Celtic from the West*, edited by Barry Cunliffe and John Koch and published by Oxbow in 2010, 2013 and 2018.

The subtitles of these volumes give you a good feel for the key themes: *Alternative Perspectives from Archaeology, Genetics, Language and Literature* (Vol. 1), *Rethinking the Bronze Age and the Arrival of Indo-European in Atlantic Europe* (Vol. 2) and *Exploring Celtic Origins: New Ways Forward in Archaeology, Linguistics and Genetics* (Vol. 3).

There is a wealth of multidisciplinary material here. If you work your way through it all, you will be very well versed on the topic!

Chapter 9

There is a wide selection of books and articles on Roman Britain generally and Roman Wales in particular. Let's run through some of the things on offer.

By now you will be familiar with Peter Salway as providing good background to Roman Britain. To the list you could add long-standing items like Frere, S., *Britannia: A History of Roman Britain*, first published 1967 (Folio Society, 1999); Mattingly, D., *An Imperial Possession: Britain in the Roman Empire 54 BC–AD 409* (Penguin, 2007) and de la Bédoyére, G., *Roman Britain: A New History* (Thames and Hudson, 2013).

There are useful references that are good to have to hand like Rivet, A. and Smith, C., *The Place-Names of Roman Britain* (Batsford, 1982); Jones, B. and Mattingly, D., *An Atlas of Roman Britain* (Oxbow, 2007); Wacher, J., *The Towns of Roman Britain* (Batsford, 1995); and Burnham, B. and Wacher, J., *The 'Small Towns' of Roman Britain* (Batsford, 1990).

Turning to Wales, you can consult Burnham, B. and Davies, J., *Conflict Co-existence and Change: Recent Work in Roman Wales*, in *Trivium*, 25 (1991); Arnold, C. and Davies, J., *Roman and Early Medieval Wales* (History Press, 2000); Davies, J. and Jones, R., *Roman Camps in*

Wales and the Marches (University of Wales Press, 2006); and Burnham, B. and Davies, J., *Roman Frontiers in Wales and the Marches* (Royal Commission, 2010). You might also like to have a look at Sherman, A. and Evans, E., *Roman Roads in South-East Wales*, GGAT report no. 2004/073 (2004).

Bringing a sharper focus on the specific sites mentioned in the text, let's start with Usk, the fortress that pre-dated Caerleon. You have already been encouraged to read things by Bill Manning. Add to that list *Report on the Excavations at Usk 1965–1971* (University of Wales Press, 1981); *Report on the Excavations at Usk 1972–1976* (University of Wales Press, 1989); and *The Fortress Excavations 1972–1974* (University of Wales Press, 1989) as well as the volumes addressing pottery and small finds.

You may also want to have a look at Marvell, A., 'Excavations at Usk 1986–1988', in *Britannia* (1996); and Marvell, A. and Maynard, D., 'Excavations South of the Legionary Fortress at Usk, Gwent, 1994', in *Britannia* (1998).

As you will have read in the text, flood-prone Usk gave way to Isca (Caerleon) and there are numerous reports that you could follow up. In fact, there is such a large body of literature that if I made any attempt to be comprehensive here, this would turn into a very long book indeed! However, we can hit a few highlights and among them are some very interesting antiquarian accounts. For example, while it may be difficult for you to find original copies, it is well worth looking at things like John Edward Lee's *Description of a Roman Building and Other Remains* (J.R. Smith, Old Compton Street, 1850) and *Isca Silurum: Or, an Illustrated Catalogue of the Museum of Antiquities at Caerleon* (Longman, 1862). A facsimile of the latter was produced in 2016. These earliest investigations were refreshingly thorough and well illustrated for their time.

Another key report, which is also quite vintage now but still important, is Wheeler, R.E.M. and Wheeler, T.V., 'The Roman Amphitheatre at Caerleon, Mon.', in *Archaaeologia*, 18 (1928).

By now, you probably feel that you have got to know Nash-Williams quite well. He's important in the context of Caerleon as well with reports of several excavations appearing in issues of *Archaeologia Cambrensis* from 1929 to 1939. A report on the Prysg Field excavations appeared in the *Bulletin of the Board of Celtic Studies* (1953). The baton was passed, figuratively speaking of course, to Lesley Murray Threipland, who published various excavations in *Archaeologia Cambrensis* between 1959 and 1965.

One of the key figures in the exploration of Caerleon was George Boon; a good starting place is his *Isca* (National Museum of Wales, 1972). This is the volume I told you about him signing that day in the pub! He also did quite a lot in Caerwent so we will be returning to him shortly.

Among the more recent investigation that you may want to read is Evans, D. and Metcalf, V., *Roman Gates* (Oxbow, 1992), especially for the later fortress, and Evans, E., *The Caerleon Canabae: Excavations in the Civil Settlement 1984–90* (Society for the Promotion of Roman Studies, 2000) in respect to the extramural developments.

To bring you right up to date, you could look at recent reports such as the geophysical investigations undertaken by Peter Guest and Tim Young published in *Archaeologia Cambrensis* in 2006 and 2009. You can also read Guest, P., Luke, M. and Pudney, C., *Archaeological Evaluation of the Extramural Monumental Complex ('The Southern Canabae') at Caerleon 2011*, Cardiff Studies in Archaeology Specialist Report 33 (2012) and Guest, P. and Gardner, A., 'Exploring Roman Caerleon: New Excavations at the Legionary Fortress of Isca', in *Archaeology International*, 12 (2009).

That's probably enough to get you started on Caerleon and to bring you up to date. Before we move on, however, something that I highly recommend to you is Zienkiewicz, D., *The Legionary Fortress Baths at Caerleon* (Cadw/National Museum of Wales, 1986).

Related material which has been particularly useful for me includes the notes and context records of the 1992 museum garden excavations (you will have to book an appointment at the National Roman Legion Museum to have a look at these) supplemented with conversations with Dave Zienkiewicz. These and the finds themselves made my articles on the tetrapylon possible – we'll come to that.

For now, let's have a look at Caerwent. As with Caerleon, to get a real feel for work in the civitas capital we need to go back a bit and look at things like Ashby, T., Hudd, A. and Martin, A., 'Excavations at Caerwent, Monmouthsire on the site of the Romano-British City of Venta Silurum in 1901', in *Archaeologia* (1902) and Ashby, T. Hudd, A. and King, F., 'Excavations at Caerwent, Monmouthshire on the site of the Romano-British City of Venta Silurum in 1907 and 1909', in *Archaeologia* (1909). The journal gives you a running commentary on excavations between 1901 and 1913.

Even if there was more than a little wall-chasing going on in these early excavations, they did provide us with a ground plan of the late town that got us started. Again, it's interesting to have a look.

For more recent and important work, there is Craster, O., 'The East Gate and Adjoining Town Wall of the Roman Town at Caerwent, Monmouthshire', in *Archaeologia Cambrensis* (1954); Casey, P., 'Caerwent (Venta Silurum): The Excavation of the North-West Corner Tower and an Analysis of the Structural Sequence of the Defences', in *Archaeologia Cambrensis* (1983); and Campbell, E. and Macdonald, P., 'Excavations at Caerwent Vicarage Orchard Garden 1973', in *Archaeologia Cambrensis* (1993).

If you have delved this deep into the suggested additional reading, you will probably also enjoy reading P.J. Casey's *The End of Roman Britain*, BAR British Series 71 (1979) and *Carausius and Allectus: The British Usurpers* (Yale, 1995).

By this point, you won't be surprised to see Victor Nash-Williams coming up again; he was active here as well. Have a look at 'Further Excavations at Caerwent, Monmouthshire, 1923–5', in *Archaeologia*, 80 (1930).

There was a *Time Team* programme from Caerwent, conducted with Wessex Archaeology, in 2009. You can read the Wessex report, Ref. 6887736 01.

Thoughout these notes I've mentioned several things that I've chosen to describe as 'game-changers'. There's a good example of one for Caerwent with the excavation of the forum basilica. Richard Brewer provides an overview in *Caerwent Roman Town* (Cadw, 2006).

Of course, there was more to the Roman military presence than the major fortresses and the civitas capital. A number of the sources already recommended to you will be helpful for the smaller forts, marching camps, etc. There isn't room to list all the relevant reports here but you could pursue things like Blockley, K., Ashmore, F. and Ashmore, P., 'Excavations on the Roman Fort at Abergavenny, Orchard Site 1972–73', in *Archaeological Journal* (1973).

Particularly important among the fort sites is Cardiff, which, as you will see in the text, ultimately superseded Isca/Caerleon. For recent work here, you could have a look at Dunning, R. *New Interpretation Centre, Cardiff Castle, Cardiff: Post Excavation Assessment 1.2*, GGAT report 2010/031 (2010).

We've already mentioned sources relating to life in the countryside such as the Thornwell Farm report. The source for the lack of nucleation mentioned in the text is Insole, P., 'A Romano-British Farmstead at Church Farm, Caldicot', in *Archaeology in Wales* (2000).

Turning to legacy and the development of the Welsh language, there are several sources you might like to read. Not surprisingly, some of the particularly useful ones are in Welsh. Examples include the now classic Lewis, H., *Datblygiad yr Iaith Gymraeg* (University of Wales Press, 1946); and, especially for regional variation, Thomas, B. and Thomas, P., *Cymraeg, Cymrág, Cymrêg: Cyflwyno'r Tafodieithoedd* (Gwasg Taf, 1989). For something in English, have a look at Davies, J., *The Welsh Language: A History* (University of Wales Press, 2014) and Ball, M. and Muller, N. (eds.), *The Celtic Languages* (Routledge, 2nd ed., 2015). The works of Rachel Bromwich are always useful. You could read *Trioedd Ynys Prydein* (University of Wales Press, 1961) and, with Jones, R., *Astuddiaethau ar yr Hengerdd* (University of Wales Press, 1978).

There is a wealth of material on the early church and on the transition from the civitates to kingdoms. For example, I have enjoyed and made good use of the books of Ken Dark. Try *Civitas to Kingdom: British Political Continuity 300–800* (Leicester, 1994) and *Discovery by Design*, BAR British Series 237 (1994).

Another must-read author is Wendy Davies, with *An Early Welsh Microcosm* (Royal Historical Society, 1978); *The Llandaff Charters* (National Library of Wales, 1979); 'Roman Settlements and Post-Roman Estates in South-East Wales', in Casey, P. (ed.), *The End of Roman Britain*, BAR British Series 237 (1979) and *Wales in the Early Middle Ages* (Leicester, 1982).

Specifically for the early church try Redknap, M., *The Christian Celts* (National Museum of Wales, 1991); Davies, D., *Celtic Christianity in Early Medieval Wales* (University of Wales Press, 2008); Petts, D., *The Early Medieval Church in Wales* (History Press, 2009); and Rees, E., *Early Christianity in South-West Britain* (Windgatherer, 2020). There is an interesting discussion of the early martyrs in Stephens, G. 'Caerleon and the Martyrdom of SS Aaron and Julius', in *Bulletin of the Board of Celtic Studies* (1985) and in Seaman, A., 'Julius and Aaron: Martyrs of Caerleon: in Search of Wales' first Christians', in *Archaeologia Cambrensis* (2015).

Don't forget George Boon. The episode with the monogram that I shared with you in the text led to 'A Christian Monogram at Caerwent', in *Bulletin of the Board of Celtic Studies* (1962) and there is an interesting discussion in 'The Early Church in Gwent: The Romano-British Church', in *Monmouthshire Antiquary* (1992).

There's more and I'll be recommending other things on this transitional period in the notes for the next chapter. But that will probably do for now!

Of special note, keep your eye out for the soon-to-be-published reports on the recent work in Caerleon and on the forum basilica excavation in Caerwent. With the former, you will want to read the ideas about the early role of Caerleon as a canabae legionis providing a pre-Caerwent administrative centre. Also have a look at the proposed medieval dating of the small building overlaying the store complex in the Priory field.

With Caerwent, the description of the very late rebuilding in parts of the basilica is very important. In several places throughout the text I've used the term 'game-changer'. That description will also apply to these reports!

Chapter 10

I've already unblushingly reminded you of my chapter on the fifth to seventh century in the *Gwent County History*; you will also want to look at Knight, J., 'Society and Religion in the Early Middle Ages'; Longley, D., 'Status and Lordship in the Early Middle Ages'; and Wood, J., 'Caerleon Restaurata: The Narrative World of Early Medieval Gwent', in that volume.

Jeremy Knight also addressed the same period for Glamorgan with 'Glamorgan AD 400–1100, Archaeology and History', and 'Sources for the Early History of Morgannwg', in Savory, H. (ed.), *The Glamorgan County History, Vol. 1* (1984).

We have already looked at sources for matters like hillfort reoccupation. Don't forget the tips regarding specific sites like Caer Dynnaf and Llwynheirnin in the notes to Chapter 7.

The classic description of the early work at Dinas Powys is Alcock, L., *Dinas Powys: An Iron Age, Dark Age and Early Medieval Settlement in Glamorgan* (University of Wales Press, 1966).

For more recent investigation and re-evaluation have a look at Gilchrist, R., 'A Reappraisal of Dinas Powys: Local Exchange and Specialised Livestock Production in Fifth- to Seventh-Century Wales', in *Medieval Archaeology* (1998).

Then you will want to turn to the work of Andy Seaman, including 'Dinas Powys in Context: Settlement and Society in Post-Roman Wales', in *Studia Celtica*, 47 (1998); and, with Lane, A., 'Excavations of Ty'n y Coed Earthworks 2011–14: the Dinas Powys "Southern Banks"', in *Archaeologia Cambrensis*, 168 (2019); and, with Sucharyna Thomas, L., 'Hillforts and Power in the British Post-Roman West: A GIS Analysis of Dinas Powys', in *European Journal of Archaeology* (2020).

There are a number of good general studies of this period. Obvious starting points are Esmonde Cleary, S., *The Ending of Roman Britain* (Batsford, 1989); Knight, J., *The End of Antiquity* (Tempus, 1991); and Higham, N., *Rome, Britain and the Anglo Saxons* (Seaby, 1992). Specifically for Wales, there is Edwards, N. and Lane, A. (eds.), *Early Medieval Settlements in Wales, AD 400–1100* (Bangor and Cardiff, 1988) and *The Early Church in Wales and the West* (Oxbow, 1992)

You would probably also like to look at a corpus including Charles-Edwards, T., *Early Irish and Welsh Kinship* (Oxford University Press, 1993) and *Wales and the Britons, 350–1064* (Oxford University press, 2013). For an up-to-date account, there is Carver, M., *Formative Britain: An Archaeology of Britain, Fifth to Eleventh Century AD* (Routledge, 2019).

If you are interested in sources, you will want to read Gildas for a primary, if more than a little irascible, account. An accessible translation is Winterbottom, M. (ed. and trans.), *The Ruin of Britain and Other Documents* (Phillimore, 1978).

You may also want to skate onto thin ice with the Book of Llandaf. The obvious starting point here is Evans, J., *Text of the Book of Llan Dâv* (National Library of Wales, 1977). Then you will want to turn to Wendy Davies, whose work has gone a long way toward making the source usable. Start with her *An Early Welsh Microcosm* (Royal Historical Society, 1978), then move on to *The Llandaff Charters* (National Library of Wales, 1979). To start putting things into perspective, you can then read *Wales in the Early Middle Ages* (Leicester University Press, 1982).

The important contribution of Wendy Davies is not the end to discussion and debate over the charters. Have a look at Davies, J.R., *The Book of Llandaf and the Norman Church in Wales* (Boydell Press, 2003); and Sims-Williams, P., *The Book of Llandaf as a Historical Source* (Boydell Press, 2019).

When you have been through all of that, you will have a good feel for the 'challenges' associated with the source. You will also have noticed that there are different views about how to spell Llandaf. It's one of those things you tend to get used to when you are dealing with Welsh place names. Just imagine the various permutations you can have in your postal address if you live in Llanfihangel tor y Mynydd! Full marks to the Post Office, by the way. My wife was once sent a letter from a friend in England directed to 'The white house on the side of the hill above the Star with the Welsh name I can't remember'. It arrived!

Chapters 11 and 12 and Conclusion

I think that we can combine the recommended reading for the remaining chapters since you have already been directed toward many of the key sources. Keep things like the recent excavations at Caerleon and the ongoing work at Caerau in mind.

You will probably find the text of *Y Gododdin*, with commentary, of interest. There are choices here but a good, accessible translation is Jarmon, A.O.H., *Aneirin – Y Gododdin* (Gwasg Gomer, Welsh Classics Series, 2005).

By now you will be well acquainted with the work of John Koch, particularly the three volumes of *Celtic from the West*. You might also want to have a look at some things more specifically addressing the origins and significance of aspects of the Mabinogi and other Welsh sources. Here's a list to get you started: 'Some Suggestions and Etymologies Reflecting upon the Mythology of the Four Branches', in *Proceedings of the Harvard Celtic Colloquium* (1989); 'A Welsh Window on the Iron Age: Manawydan, Mandubracios', in *Cambridge Medieval Studies* (1987); 'Gleanings from the Gododdin and Other Early Welsh Texts', in *Bulletin of the Board of Celtic Studies* (1991); and 'On Celts Calling Themselves "Celts" and Related Questions', in *Studia Celtica* (2009).

A 'hot-off-the-press' item (or at the time of writing, almost off the press – I've read the proofs) looking for Iron Age roots in later traditions is Olding, F., 'The Gods of Gwent: Iron Age and Romano-British Deities in South-East Wales', in *Monmouthshire Antiquary*, 35 (2021).

I mentioned at the outset that we would want to think about translations, and this is a good spot at which to do so. In the first book specifically about the Silures, I raised an issue about the translation of the description of the Silures in the Agricola – *Silurum colorati vultus*, etc. The specific point I raised was about the nebulous possible translations of *coloratus* – there are a number.

This raised questions in my mind about how much easier it would have been for Tacitus to say *fuscus vultus* to convey the now standard 'swarthy-faced' translation. I even suggested, not entirely tongue in cheek, that *coloratus* could even refer to war paint! I'm not trying to tell you that it did. I'm simply noting how important it is to return to source with such written evidence – especially if the source is in another language.

Moving on, the cluster model that is mentioned in the text can be found in Lancaster, J., 'A Model of Decentralised Political Structure Amongst the Silures', in *Studia Celtica* (2014).

I suspect that I began this further reading list in bad form by recommending a couple of my own things. We may as well finish on a similar note. My investigation and interpretation of the destruction of the tetrapylon in Caerleon, arising from Dave Zienkiewicz's excavation, is in large part a bit late for this book. However, I think it relates and I find it very interesting.

Consequently, you might like to have a look at Howell, R., 'The Demolition of the Roman Tetrapylon in Caerleon: An Erasure of Memory?', in *Oxford Journal of Archaeology* (2000) and/or 'Roman Survival — Welsh Revival: the Evidence of Reuse of Roman Remains', in *The Monmouthshire Antiquary* (2001).

There are some things to be getting on with. Apologies for anything that I have left out, especially to any colleagues whose important contributions have been overlooked. On the bright side, if you do decide to work through the reading materials suggested above, and chase the appropriate references, you'll find anything I've missed out anyway.

So, I'll just say happy hunting!

Appendix

As I've explained in the text, this book is in part a product of the lockdown during much of 2020. When this pandemic problem began, I was on the verge of starting a new research initiative using computer mapping, working with colleagues Giles Oatley and Simon Maddison. I devised a preliminary model to help us refine our research design and we were on the verge of a bit of fieldwork, drone photography, etc. As I explain in the main text, this seems to be a good area of research that can be facilitated relatively easily without any injection of grant funding. Unfortunately, things are still on hold as I write this, but we hope to resume investigations when conditions permit.

In the meanwhile, here is the initial plan that I sent to colleagues to get the ball rolling. It is far from a finished product and, as I hope the document makes clear, is one that will undoubtedly develop and change as our investigations proceed. I hope, however, that it is a paper that can form the basis for an investigation and it is one that shows the way I am thinking about this distribution pattern at the moment. Consequently, you may find it interesting and/or useful. I haven't tidied it and it contains comments intended for my co-researchers. Hopefully you may find that interesting as well. So, here it is, 'warts and all'.

Hillfort clusters: preliminary model

In order to establish a structure for further investigation, I have grouped the hillforts listed by the *Atlas* into possible clusters. Wanting to establish a manageable study area in the first instance, this listing concentrates on the area between Usk and Wye. The coast defines the southern limit while the northern boundary, that at present extends into the Black Mountains, may require some modification as analysis develops.

This preliminary model suggests seven clusters, although these may overlap in such a way that the number should be reduced. For example, I initially considered an Olwy (not a very precise description) cluster and a Middle Usk cluster. On reflection, however, at the moment it seems best to treat this as one larger cluster. On the other hand, this model proposes Lower Usk East and West clusters. It seems likely that there would have been a close relationship between the two. Similarly, Lower Usk East seems closely associated with what, at the moment, I'm calling a Llanmelin cluster. It's difficult, for example, to say if the Castell Prin site, now in Lower Usk East might sit more comfortably in Llanmelin. Similar questions arise between Llanmelin and Lower Wye, Lower Wye and Olwy-Lower Usk Clusters, etc. No doubt these are among the issues to be considered in subsequent investigations.

The clusters range in size from four to six hillforts with a fairly coherent-looking mix of larger and smaller sites. The proposed clusters and associated hillforts are listed below with information derived from the *Atlas* and in a few instances other sources including field visit. I've noted references referred to in the *Atlas*.

Lower Wye Cluster

WA 2412 Piercefield Great Camp (Pierce Wood Camp)

HER 00772g (Glamorgan–Gwent unless otherwise indicated)
NMR ST59NW
SM MM53639
ST 53639
- Described as an oblong contour hillfort on a spur 388m x 110m; 4.16ha internal area; inturned entrance with corridor and guard chambers.
- Refs: Gerrard et al. (2006) – This is the GGAT Prehistoric Defended Enclosure report that is discussed below.
- The site is in woods on the Wye Valley Walk north of the Piercefield House ruins.

WA 2417 Piercefield Little Camp (Piercewood Camp)

(called Lower Camp on Megalithic portal)
HER 01193g
NMR ST59NW35
SM MM020A
ST 532595
- Small site (outpost?) 'short distance W. from Piercefield Great Camp', 98m x 82m; 0.72ha.
- Refs: Gerrard et al. (2006)

WA 2406 Gaer Hill Camp, Penterry

(it's actually nearer to St Arvans)
HER 00745g
NMR ST 59 NW6
SM MM025
ST 51709
- Described as contour hillfort with two widely spaced ramparts 240m x 254m; large outer enclosure 'possible multiple enclosure' 0.57ha and 4.5ha; simple gap entrances SW and NE.
- This is the one with the transmission mast just above St Arvans.

WA 2408 Blackfield Wood Camp (Porthcaseg Camp)

HER 00748g
NMR ST59NW
SM MM027
ST 52909

- Described as a triangular 'inland promontory' fort 90m x 50m; 0.46ha; simple gap entrance SW.
- Refs: Eden (2000), Gerrard et al. (2006). Eden did a soil study for a Bristol dissertation.
- Porthcaseg is the name of the farm.

WA 2430 The Bulwarks, Chepstow

HER 01193
NMR ST59SW
SM MM093
ST53799

- Described as a bivallate inland promontory fort 104m x 120m; 1.2ha; simple gap entrance SW.
- Refs: Savory (1950), Whittle (1992), Gerrard et al. (2006). Savory is a list of hillforts in the *Bulletin of the Board of Celtic Studies* – Whittle a wider study for HMSO.

EN 4148 Lancaut (Spittal Meend)

HER Gloucestershire 23 (this site is east of the river but looks to be associated with the Piercefield camps – closest site to the east is Lydney)
NMR ST59NW3
SM 1004858
ST 54226

- Two banks with ditches cutting off promontory to E measuring (less than helpfully) 37m overall; simple gap entrance E.
- Refs: Barker et al (2000), Hoyle and Vallender (Offa's Dyke Management Survey, 1995), and the Offa's Dyke Field survey undertaken by Fox (1955). The most useful things here might be a geophysical survey undertaken by STRATOSCAN (unpublished report 1458) and a report of three assessment trenches dug by Rehion Archaeological Services.
- The *Atlas* refers to the site's proximity to 'Bang y Gor' – this is actually Ban y Gor.
- *Olwy-Middle Usk Cluster*

WA 2424 Trelech Gaer (Gaer hillfort)

(says Trellech but one l is more correct)
HER 00972g
NMR SO40SE25
SM MM077
SO 49300

- Isolated sub-circular hillfort with possible annex 32m x 35m; 0.25ha; entrance oblique SW.
- Refs: Savory (1950), Howell (2006), Gerard et al. (2006) (I did little more than mention it in Silures).
- The *Atlas* notes that this site is located 'at the headwater of a stream tributary of the River Usk'.

WA 2439 Mitchel Troy Enclosure

HER 08941g
NMR SO41SW
SM -----
SO 49010

- This is described as an unconfirmed 'little known possible site' on a SE facing spur above the Trothy. There is no information regarding size but the *Atlas* notes three banks with 'ditches only visible on NW side'.
- Refs: Gerrard et al. (2006)

WA 2423 Great House Camp

HER 00942
NMR SO40SW 23
SM MM105
SO 432240
- Described as an isolated, multivallate contour hillfort at NE end of ridge above the Olwy Valley with four banks and ditches and inner revetment; 140m x 150m; 2.56ha; entrances simple gap N and S.
- Ref: Gerrard et al. (2006)
- This is near Llansoy. I have a copy of Mark Belcher's long essay based on geophysics here. The hillfort is described in the *Atlas* as isolated but it doesn't seem very isolated to me. I've always thought of it 'working in tandem' with Gaer Fawr.

WA 2428 Gaer Fawr Camp, Llangwm

HER 01131g.
NMR ST49NW19
SM MM062
ST 44149
- Described as a large, oblong contour hillfort in a 'commanding position on N-S spur in hills above the River Usk', it has three ramparts S & W and two ('much eroded') E. Dimensions are not given and the entrance is 'unknown'. However, the internal area is put at 6.9ha.
- Refs: Savory (1950), Howell (2006), Gerrard et al. (2006).

WA 2438 Coed y Bwynydd Camp (Coed y Bwnyff)

HER 0217g
NMR SO30NE 36
SM MM075
SO 365068
- Multivallate contour hillfort on S tip of Clytha Hill above River Usk; 170m x 114 m; 1.22ha; inturned entrance with guard chambers NE.
- Refs: Savory (1950), Babbidge (1977)* [this is the excavation report], Whittle (1992), Howell (2006), Gerrard et al. (2006). I've discussed the site with Adrian Babbidge, who directed the excavation.

WA 2437 Llancayo Camp (Campswood; Camp Wood)

HER 02166g
NMR SO30SE
SM MM078
SO 378038
- Described as a large, oval contour hillfort at the end of Llancayo Ridge above bends in the River Usk with a 'substantial bank and ditch that follows contours' and 'an

impressive entrance SE'. For some reason, no dimensions are given in the *Atlas* but Coflein puts it at 285m x 140m.
- Refs: Savory (1950).
- This one is near Trostrey.

Llanmelin Cluster

WA 2426 Llanmelin Wood Camp and Llanmelin Outpost, Caerwent

HER 01026g
NMR ST49SE1
SM MM024
ST 461092
- This is one of our most important sites, in part because it is one of the most fully excavated. It is multivallate; 230m x 150m; 1.32ha; with annexe(s) 40 m x 21m. The smaller C-shaped outpost is to the NE; inturned entrance SE; annexe entrance only to the 'outermost one'.
- Refs: Nash-Williams (1933) [the excavation report], Savory (1950), Forde Johnson (1976), Whittle (1992).
- Issues relating to such things as the annexe(s) are interesting and challenging. The reference list is incomplete. Particularly important is the MPhil thesis of Daryl Williams, who did extensive geophysical investigation here along with other surveys at Coed y Caerau and Gaer Fawr.

WA 2429 Sudbrook Camp

HER 01142
NMR ST58NW
SM NN048
ST 505587
- An important multivallate coastal promontory fort: 200m x 92m; 1.37ha. This is another important site because it also was excavated by Nash-Williams with subsequent re-investigations. The dimensions are probably deceptive because there is very substantial coastal erosion and a presumed loss of much of the site.
- Refs: Nash-Williams (1938) [the excavation report], Savory (1950), Hogg (1965), Whittle (1992), Sell (2001) [limited re-excavation].

WA 1556 Wilcrick Camp

HER 00474g
NMR ST48NW
SM MM127
ST 411187
- Described as an oval multivallate contour hillfort on an 'isolated prominent hill above the coastal plain'; 194m x 134m; 2ha; with an entrance ('overlapping') and corridor NE as well as a hollow way SW.
- Refs: Savory (1950), Howell (2006).

WA 1792 The Larches Camp

HER 00473g
NMR ST 48NW17
SM MM069
ST43298

- The description here is of a small, roughly circular contour hillfort on Grange Wood hilltop above the coastal plain with single bank and ditch and an inturned entrance W; 52m x 46m; 0.24ha.
- Refs: Savory (1950).

Lower Usk East Cluster

(might be less confusing to call it the Lodge Hill Cluster?)

WA 1800 Lodge Wood Camp (Lodge Hill Camp; Belinstock)

HER 00597g
NMR ST39SW
SM MM023
ST 323091

- This is the site that we dug as a result of funding for a millennium project. It's 400m x 800m; 2.2ha; entrances are oblique SE, blocked with guard chambers W.
- Refs: Coxe (1801), Savory (1950), Whittle (1992), Howell (2006), Pollard et al. (2006), Gerrard et al. (2006).
- This is an interesting one for several reasons including the ceramic assemblage (briquetage, etc.), evidence of reoccupation, the blocked entrance (reopened at some point late in the sequence, etc. Not surprisingly, I have the excavation report *Lodge Hill Camp, Caerleon and the Hillforts of Gwent*, Pollard, Howell, Chadwick and Leaver, BAR British Series 407.

WA 1598 St. Julian's Wood Camp Christchurch

HER 00220g
NMR ST38NW
SM MM021
ST 339938

- Described as a possible but unconfirmed small sub-rectangular hillslope fort with 'faint evidence of banks and ditches'; no dimensions given.
- This one, assuming it is there, is on the opposite bank from Lodge Hill.

WA 4353 Coed y Caerau Enclosure Complex

HER 00414g, 00415g 00416g.
NMR ST39SE39
ST 378991

- The description here is of a three bivallate or univallate conjoined site. The nature of the site, as well as the inclination of some to try to disarticulate it into separate but conjoined sites leads to the complex numbering/naming system. Some describe the middle enclosure as Pen Toppen Ash. Dimensions are given as: SW (part bivallate) 84m x 94m; 0.8ha – Centre 74m x 8m; 0.6ha – SW 136m x 142m; 1.9ha.

- Refs: The only reference in the *Atlas* is to Wiggins (2006) – the GGAT survey. I think more important is Daryl's report of the geophysics. Daryl was one of my postgraduate students and we both think the most plausible interpretation is Iron Age A, B, possibly C, Roman (the end enclosure is square and looks a lot like a small fortlet/signal station). Only one way to find out!

WA 2399 Caerau Camp, Ponthir

HER 00645g
NMR ST39SW28
SM MM 135
ST 329893

- Described as a small circular univallate contour hillfort above the Afon Llwyd 'opposite to Lodge Hill'. Dimensions not given apart from a possible internal area of 0.48ha.
- Refs: Savory (1950), Gerard et al. (2006).

WA 1645 Cae Camp

HER 00387g
NMR ST39SE13
SM MM079
ST359093

- Cae Camp is described as a suboval contour hillfort 'above bend of the River Usk and the Sorbrook' with simple gap entrance SE; 92m x 65m; 0.5ha.
- Refs: Savory (1950).

WA2425 Castell Prin

HER 01022g
NMR ST49SW34
SM MM130
ST 409892

- A sub-rectangular contour hillfort with inturned entrance S; 70m x 34m; 0.24ha.
- Refs: Gerrard et al. (2006)
- I'm still a bit in two minds with this one. A case could be made for putting it in the Llanmelin Cluster – but I suppose that's one of the sorts of things we can look at.

Lower Usk West Cluster

WA 1507 Tredegar Camp

HER 00049g
NMR ST28NE
SM MM084
ST289586

- Described as a multivallate contour hillfort above the Ebbw and the mouth of the Usk with a simple gap entrance SE; inner enclosure 142m x 70m; 4.65ha with 0.9ha annexe.
- Refs: Savory (1950), Houlder (1978), Whittle (1992), Gerrard et al. (2006). Carolyn Martin, one of my undergraduates, did some survey work here and subsequently after she went to Cardiff as a postgraduate.

WA 1509 Graig y Saeson (Y Gaer, Coed y Defaid)

HER 00057g
NMR ST28NE14
SM MM 134
ST 273386
- A small univallate angular contour hillfort above the confluence of the River Ebbw and the mouth of the Usk; 80m x 70 m; 0.52ha.
- Refs: Savory (1950), Gerrard et al. (2006)

WA 1497 The Mount, Pen y Lan (Pen y Parc Newydd, Pen y Lan Camp)

HER 00005g
NMR ST28SE1
SM MM133
ST 258584
- A small, partly bivallate hilltop contour hillfort above the coastal plain and the confluence of the Ebbw and Uskmouth; 80m x 62m; 0.48ha.
- Refs: Savory (1950), Whittle (1992), Gerrard et al. (2006).

WA 1505 Rhiwderin Camp

HER 00039g
NMRST 28 NE 1
SM MM066
ST 264087
- A small univallate contour hillfort on a knoll above the Ebbw; *c.* 80m x 60m; no internal estimate as the site is 'almost destroyed'.
- Refs: Savory (1950).

There are a number of questions emerging. One is the relationship between the Lower Usk Cluster and sites to the west like WA 2434 Ruperra (nr. Caerffili) and WA 2398 Castle Field Camp, Graig Llwyn. If we stick with the Usk/Wye initial study area, more immediate is how Lower Wye E and W, Llanmelin, and Lower Wye might relate. For example, are all of these parts of a lowland/coastal zone?

Black Mountains East Cluster

WA 2432 Ysgyryd (Skirrid) Fawr

HER 01497g
NMR SO31NW
SM MM182
SO 331118
- This site is confirmed as a feature but described as a possible contour hillfort with a medieval dimension; 320m x 100m; 3.2ha.
- Refs: Savory (1950), Gerrard et al. (2006)
- This is a dominating location but interpretation is 'challenging'. There are three low banks and ditches N, S, and W but as the *Atlas* points out, the St Michael's chapel earthworks 'cause confusion'.

WA 2435 Twyn y Gaer, Llanfihangel Crucorney

HER 01713g
NMR SO22SE
SM MM148
SO 294021

- Described as a commanding excavated contour hillfort with crossbanks and ditches dividing the interior into three parts. This may be why dimensions are not given apart from an interior area of 1.8ha. There is a simple gap entrance E and a passageway/corridor W.
- Refs: Savory (1950), Probert (1976) [This National Museum compendium is the closest we have to an excavation report], Whittle (1992), Howell (2006), Gerrard et al. (2006).
- This is a potentially important site that unfortunately, while having been excavated, hasn't been fully written up. The notes are in the National Museum but, as Alan Probert died several years ago, probably won't be published in any more detail than the 1976 summary. I had a chance to talk to him about the excavations several times – he was convinced that phasing saw a reduction in the size of the hillfort. He had a notion of a smaller 'Silurian' style replacing a larger 'Dubunnic' one. We should keep the idea in mind as it could be a factor in characterising the Cluster and interpreting the sites east of Twyn y Gaer.

WA 2433 Pen Twyn, Llanfihangel Crucorney

HER 01607g
NMR SO32SW6
SM MM064
SO 321123

- The *Atlas* description is of a commanding oblong contour hillfort on the S end of Hatteral Hill above the confluence of the Honddu and the Monnow. The further suggestion is that it, along with Crug Hywel and Twyn y Gaer, guards the S end of three of the four ridges of the Black Mountains. It is multivallate but may have started as univallate; 140m x 70m; 3.28ha.
- Refs: Gerrard et al. (2006).

EN Walterstone Camp

(Coed y Grafel)
HER Herefordshire MHE804
NMR SO32NW3
SM 100 1755
SO 348250

- A roughly circular triple-banked contour hillfort with simple gap entrance SW; dimensions not given but internal area put at 1.77ha.
- Refs: RCHME (1931), Dorling and Wigley (2012).

Walterstone and the two other Herefordshire sites that follow should, perhaps, be looked at keeping Probert's idea about Twyn y Gaer in mind.

EN 0027 Penapark (Pen y Parc)

HER Herefordshire 10360
No NMR/ SM given
SO 383257
- Described as a large triple-banked enclosure defined mainly by cropmarks on a ridge overlooking the Monnow Valley with a simple gap enclosure; area not defined.
- Ref: Dorling and Wigley (2012).

EN0006 Broad Oak, Garway

HER Herefordshire MHE 21869
No NMR/SM
SO 436244
- Status described as 'irreconciled issues' – possible inland promontory fort 'ploughed for centuries'; 'no access, area not determined'.

The Herefordshire sites appear as dots on the *Atlas* map and seem to relate to Twyn y Gaer, etc. However, the lack of information, particularly relating to the last two, makes them problematic.

Black Mountains West Cluster

WA 1474 Crug Hywel (Crucywel)

HER Clwyd Powys 1057
NMR SO22SW
SM BR128 (POW)
SO 225520
- Described as a high prominent partial contour hillfort on SE slopes of Table Mountain overlooking River Usk at its confluence with the Grwyne Fawr and Grwyne Fechan with inturned entrance SE; 100m x 50m; 0.72ha.
- Refs: Savory (1952), RCAHMW (1986), Silvester (2007) [CPAT No. 859].

WA 1222 Llangenny Camp

HER Clwyd Powys 695
NMR SO~21NW12
SM BR061 (POW)
SO 228118
- Univallate contour hillfort above River Usk with simple gap entrances E and NW; 70m x 52m; 0.29ha.
- Refs: RCAHMW (1986), Silvester (2007).

WA 1450 Pen Ffawyddog Gaer

(The three alternative names in the *Atlas* data base are simply awful misspellings of the original – don't think we need them)
HER Clwyd Powys 1057
NMR SO11NE5
SM BR060 (POW)
SO 195718

- A small univallate hillslope fort above a bend in the River Usk with a simple gap entrance NW; 57m x 74m; 0.45ha.
- Refs: Savory (1952), RCAHMW (1986), Silvester (2007).

WA 1211 Coed Pentwyn (Coed Pen-Twyn)

HER Clwyd Powys 3342
NMR SO11NE6
SM BR190 (POW)
SO193516

- Described as a large bivallate heart-shaped partial contour fort on Mynydd Llangatwg above the River Usk at Crickhowell with an inturned entrance, passageway-corridor NE; 138m x 75m; 0.29ha. (hard to see how this is large!?!)
- Refs: RCAHMW (1986), Silvester (2007).

WA 1332 Coed y Gaer, Llanfihangel Cwmdu

HER Clwyd Powys 660
NMR SO12SE8

- SM BR 115 A small partial contour fort overlooking a possible route from the River Usk to the River Wye via the Rhiangoll (toward Talgarth) with a simple gap entrance W.
- Refs: as above

With respect to the route from Usk to Wye, the *Atlas* notes that going toward Talgarth/ Three Cocks it is 'hillforts all the way'. There does seem to be the hint of a 'system' or relationship based on topography in this cluster that leaps out at you more than some of the others. That may simply be because the topography is more extreme in the mountains.

WA 1333 Penmyarth Camp

(saved this one for last since, if these dimensions are right, it's a monster!)
(Myarth Camp)
HER Clwyd Powys 664
NMR SO12SE
SM BR116 (POW)
SO 172020

- The status of this one is 'confirmed' but the description says possible large contour hillfort on the summit of Myarth 'commanding a potential route from the River Usk to the River Wye' that 'dominates a narrow stretch of the middle Usk Valley'. RCAHMW (1973–82) reported no traces of earthworks at a site 'heavily disturbed and afforested with linear mining'. However, Savory, who visited in 1947, reported a bivallate fort with a deep inturned entrance ESE, and in 1988 CPAT (Silvester et al.) reported a length of double rampart, which was subsequently confirmed by an aerial survey by RCAHMW. The dimensions are put at 354m x 210m; 12ha!

This concludes the preliminary initial model but there are a lot of hillforts up here, beyond to N Mynydd Llangorse, Castell Dinas (Talgarth), Pendre (Talgarth), etc. and to the E & W Allt yr Esgair, Cross Oak Powys, Tumpwood Camp, Clydach, Nant Tarthwynni, etc. We'll need to decide how big a first bite we want to take.

One final entry from the *Atlas* that, although beyond the presently defined limits of Lower Usk West, is so dominant that it's hard to ignore.

WA 1545 Twmbarlwm

HER 00114g
NMR ST29SW
SM MM044
ST 242179

- A univallate 'high and commanding contour' hillfort directly above the Ebbw and its confluence with the Sirhowy rivers (fawr and fechan); 330m x 135m. No internal dimension is given but Coflein says 4.14ha.
- Ref: Whittle (1992) [I recently wrote a short piece on the site for Frank Oldling's latest book].
- As noted, if things like line of sight are taken into account it's hard to ignore Twmbarlwm − you can see a long way in all directions from the top!

Hopefully this provides a model/framework that can inform our strategy for taking this forward. There is one (at least) potential complication that we will need to consider early on. Here goes.

In 2006 GGAT published the results of its Cadw-funded Prehistoric Defended Enclosures in Gwent survey [GGAT report no. 2006/021 − Project no. GGAT 78]. A number of possible sites including a category called definite and probable were mapped. Some of these seem a bit speculative to me but there are sites like Hatterall Hill (GGAT no. 08958g/ SO30762554) that, based on a desktop assessment, is reported as a univallate defended site with a simple entrance. These seem less problematic. In the proposed study area, there are a 'lucky' thirteen sites that would impact on most of the clusters, particularly Olwy-Middle Usk.

Maybe if one of our objectives is to look for additional sites based on spatial associations developed in the study, checking against the GGAT listings might become an aspect of that phase of the investigation. Certainly, trying to devise criteria for incorporating these sites from the outset would complicate things (a lot, I think). Anyway, something to consider.

Index

You may also enjoy …

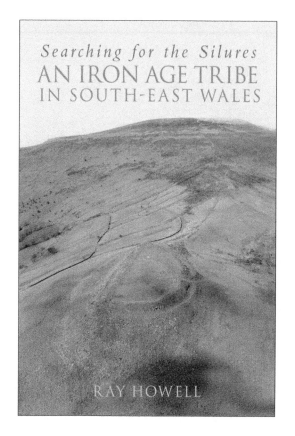

Searching for the Silures
AN IRON AGE TRIBE
IN SOUTH-EAST WALES

9780752440149

The story of the Silures is one of the most grip-
ping to have come down to us from later British
prehistory – and this fully illustrated account
from Dr Ray Howell tells that story·